# ASP
## Safety Fundamentals Exam
# SECRETS

## Study Guide
### Your Key to Exam Success

ASP Test Review for the
Associate Safety Professional Exam

Dear Future Exam Success Story:

Congratulations on your purchase of our study guide. Our goal in writing our study guide was to cover the content on the test, as well as provide insight into typical test taking mistakes and how to overcome them.

Standardized tests are a key component of being successful, which only increases the importance of doing well in the high-pressure high-stakes environment of test day. How well you do on this test will have a significant impact on your future, and we have the research and practical advice to help you execute on test day.

The product you're reading now is designed to exploit weaknesses in the test itself, and help you avoid the most common errors test takers frequently make.

### How to use this study guide

We don't want to waste your time. Our study guide is fast-paced and fluff-free. We suggest going through it a number of times, as repetition is an important part of learning new information and concepts.

First, read through the study guide completely to get a feel for the content and organization. Read the general success strategies first, and then proceed to the content sections. Each tip has been carefully selected for its effectiveness.

Second, read through the study guide again, and take notes in the margins and highlight those sections where you may have a particular weakness.

Finally, bring the manual with you on test day and study it before the exam begins.

### Your success is our success

We would be delighted to hear about your success. Send us an email and tell us your story. Thanks for your business and we wish you continued success.

Sincerely,

Mometrix Test Preparation Team

**Need more help? Check out our flashcards at: http://MometrixFlashcards.com/CSP**

Copyright © 2014 by Mometrix Media LLC. All rights reserved.
Written and edited by the Mometrix Exam Secrets Test Prep Team
Printed in the United States of America

# TABLE OF CONTENTS

# Top 20 Test Taking Tips

1. Carefully follow all the test registration procedures
2. Know the test directions, duration, topics, question types, how many questions
3. Setup a flexible study schedule at least 3-4 weeks before test day
4. Study during the time of day you are most alert, relaxed, and stress free
5. Maximize your learning style; visual learner use visual study aids, auditory learner use auditory study aids
6. Focus on your weakest knowledge base
7. Find a study partner to review with and help clarify questions
8. Practice, practice, practice
9. Get a good night's sleep; don't try to cram the night before the test
10. Eat a well balanced meal
11. Know the exact physical location of the testing site; drive the route to the site prior to test day
12. Bring a set of ear plugs; the testing center could be noisy
13. Wear comfortable, loose fitting, layered clothing to the testing center; prepare for it to be either cold or hot during the test
14. Bring at least 2 current forms of ID to the testing center
15. Arrive to the test early; be prepared to wait and be patient
16. Eliminate the obviously wrong answer choices, then guess the first remaining choice
17. Pace yourself; don't rush, but keep working and move on if you get stuck
18. Maintain a positive attitude even if the test is going poorly
19. Keep your first answer unless you are positive it is wrong
20. Check your work, don't make a careless mistake

Copyright © Mometrix Media. You have been licensed one copy of this document for personal use only. Any other reproduction or redistribution is strictly prohibited. All rights reserved.

# Business Principles, Practices, and Metrics

## Time value of money

When money is invested in a safe banking type institution, it can accumulate or accrue interest. The amount of interest earned is called the accrued amount. The interest amount is based on the amount of the investment, the length of time it is invested, and the interest percentage rate. If the money is invested over several time cycles then the interest is calculated differently. At the end of each time cycle the interest is calculated on the increased investment amount which is known as compounded interest. The effective interest rate is the interest rate between compounding cycles. If the effective interest rate is calculated over a year it is known as the effective annual interest rate.

## Cash flow and cash flow diagrams

The analysis of money going in and out of an entity is cash flow. If the rent is due on Thursday and you are paid on Friday, you have a cash flow problem. All cash flow analysis is dependent upon the business entity of interest. A cash flow out from one business entity is a cash flow in for another entity. Paying the rent is a cash flow out for the renter but is an inflow of cash for the landlord. A cash flow diagram is a chart with the horizontal axis of time with money coming in as an up arrow and money going out as a down arrow. At any point in time, the sum of cash in and out can be represented by individual arrows or a single arrow with the sum. Money cash flow can be a single payment, a uniform series of equal values of money at regular time intervals, or gradient series of increasing or decreasing values of money at regular time intervals.

## Functional notation

There are many discount tables that convert cash flows from one type to another equivalent type. The names for these tables are not standardized and take many characters to identify so a short hand version has been devised known as functional notation. Function notation uses a three terms separated by commas between parentheses. The first term indicates the first letter of the type of cash flow you are starting with and the type of cash flow you wish to calculate separated by a vertical line. The four cash flows are identified by Present (P), Future (F), Annual (A), or Gradient (G). The second term of the functional notation is the interest rate and the third term is the number of cycles. If you want the discount factor for present value given a future value at five percent annual interest rate for four years, you would look for the (P|F,5%,4) discount factor.

## Discount factors and equivalence

A technique for comparing various cash flows is the use of discount factors. The comparison of cash flows can be done at the current time called the present worth or it can be done at some time later known as the future worth. Cash flows can also be compared on an annual amount basis. There are tables of discount factors for one time cash flows in or out known as single payment compound amount factor. There are also discount factor tables for cash flows that repeat and are known either known as uniform series if the

- 2 -

Copyright © Mometrix Media. You have been licensed one copy of this document for personal use only. Any other reproduction or redistribution is strictly prohibited. All rights reserved.

amount is unchanging or gradient series if the amounts increase or decrease over time. When you calculate present or future worth of two or more cash flows and they are the same value then the cash flows are equivalent. Typically equivalence is not the goal of cash flow calculations; normally you are trying to minimize negative cash flows or maximizing positive cash flows.

## Continuous compounding

For almost all normal investment or loan situations, interest is calculated on a discrete time basis such as monthly, quarterly, or yearly. The discrete compound interest discount factors can be found in tables. There are some situations that the interest is compounded everyday, such as credit cards where purchases are made while there is an outstanding balance. Compounding interest everyday or more often is known as continuous compound interest. The continuous interest discount factors are not normally listed in tables and can be calculated using exponential equations using the nominal interest rate, r, and the time period in years, n.

## Discontinuous and random compounding

Normally interest on an investment or a loan is compounded on some recurring basis thus it is called compound interest. This recurring basis may or may not be an annual time period. If it is not annual then it is simply known as the nominal interest rate or for money invested in banks it is sometimes referred to as the yield, identified by r. Between the periods of compounding, interest may be calculated on the investment or loan amount. The effective interest rate, identified as i, is the nominal interest rate divided by the number of time periods between the compound time periods.

## Book value

The book value, BV, is a calculated amount that starts with the purchase price and subtracts the accumulated depreciation or the sum of all the depreciations, regardless of how the depreciation is calculated. The book value is normally calculated at the end of each year although some companies apply depreciation on a monthly basis. The original book value is the same as the purchase price until depreciation is applied whether that is a month or at the end of the end whichever is used by the company. The book value or the ratio of the book value to the initial purchase price is used by many depreciation schemes.

## Straight line and accelerated depreciation

For most people, depreciation is the decrease in value in a piece of equipment due to use or misuse over time. For the Internal Revenue Service, depreciation is the calculated annual expense that takes a single large purchase and distributes it over several years. The current tax laws, type of purchase and amount determines how large a purchase has to be to be depreciated and how it should be calculated. First the depreciation basis must be calculated which is the purchase price minus the salvage value. The simplest depreciation calculation is called the straight-line depreciation method which uses the depreciation basis divided by the number of years between the purchase and the salvage time. The Accelerated Cost Recovery System (ACRS) or the Modified Accelerated Cost Recovery System (MACRS) uses a series of factors to determine the amount of depreciation each year. Depreciation is in

*Copyright © Mometrix Media. You have been licensed one copy of this document for personal use only. Any other reproduction or redistribution is strictly prohibited. All rights reserved.*

engineering economics because comparing similar purchases may have different depreciation basis or depreciation schedules.

**Capitalized cost**

Capitalized cost is the present worth of an infinitely long cash flow scenario that requires no other expenses to continue the scenario by way of compound interest. The idea is if you had the entire capitalized cost sitting in the bank earning interest, the project would never run out of money. The discount factors for infinite time periods are not listed but the present value of an infinite series is the equivalent uniform annual cost (EUAC) divided by the interest rate. Since capitalized cost is expenses, a negative number means that incoming future money exceeds the cost of the cash flow scenario which is typical in commercial ventures but rarely occurs with large infrastructure projects.

**EUAC**

Besides comparing the value or cost of various cash flows at present or future worth, there is another common technique known as the Equivalent Uniform Annual Cost or EUAC. Where present or future worth provide positive values for incoming monies and negative values for outgoing monies, the EUAC is a cost so positive values are for outgoing monies and negative values for incoming monies. The EUAC is useful for comparing large infrastructure projects that may have very different lifetimes. The Equivalent Uniform Annual Cost, as it sounds, is the sum of all the negative cash flows minus the sum of all the positive cash flows divided by the number of years the cash flows occur.

**Alternative economic comparisons**

Rarely engineering projects have no design tradeoffs. When the outcomes of these design tradeoffs produce similar results then the preferred approach must be selected using some form of economic analysis. There are five normal economic comparison tools commonly used with pros and cons for each tool. The comparisons are Present Worth Analysis which simply looks for the maximum present worth of competing scenarios, Annual Cost Analysis which simply looks for the minimum EUAC, Rate of Return Analysis which looks for the highest interest rate, Benefit-Cost Analysis which looks at where benefits for different users and cost to all, and Break Even Analysis which looks at the shortest time until the project pays for itself.

**Bond, face value, date of maturity, bond value, and yield**

A bond is a financial agreement usually between an investor and a government entity that promises the government entity will repay the principal plus interest at a certain set time usually long term in nature. Face value is a bond's stated principal amount. Usually bonds are purchased for an amount lower than the face value. Some bonds continue to accrue interest beyond the face value. Date of maturity is the agreed upon date when a bond attains the face value. For some bonds, the interest may continue to earn interest after this date. Bond value is, at any time, the redeemable value of the bond. Yield is the nominal interest rate for a bond including the original purchase price, any interest earned, as well as the final value when the bond is redeemed.

*Copyright © Mometrix Media. You have been licensed one copy of this document for personal use only. Any other reproduction or redistribution is strictly prohibited. All rights reserved.*

## Benefit cost analysis

One of the five common economic comparisons is the benefit cost analysis. Of the five economic comparison techniques, the benefit cost analysis is easily the most complicated to perform and is also most subjective in nature. In simple terms, the benefit cost analysis looks at where benefits will occur for different users and total cost to everyone. Benefit cost analysis is not normally applied to commercial projects unless they are extremely large and is normally applied to government projects. The sum of the benefits divided by the sum of the costs should be greater than one for an acceptable project. When comparing multiple projects, the highest ratio will determine the best project. The exact sum of benefits and costs are sometimes difficult to accurately determine – a benefit to one group may be a cost to another group.

## Break even analysis

One of the five common economic comparisons is break even analysis. In the simplest terms, break even analysis looks at the shortest time or minimum number of units until the project pays for itself. This analysis is sometimes known as determining the pay back period. To use break even analysis, the projects must have costs and generate revenue so this is usually limited to commercial ventures and not government infrastructure projects. If a project ends before the break even or pay back occurs then the project will be a net loss for the company. At any time after the break even occurs, the company will expect a new profit.

## Rate of return cost analysis

One of the five common economic comparisons is the rate of return cost analysis or simply known as ROR. The Rate of Return Analysis looks for the highest interest rate of competing cash flow projection scenarios. A simpler definition is how much interest would I earn if I put that amount of money in a bank and coincidentally that is also a measure of whether you should do a project is would the money have been better off sitting in a bank instead of risked on this venture. This minimum acceptable interest rate is known as the minimum attractive rate of return or MARR and is established by the company. Some companies use different MARR values for different projects or project lengths.

## Present worth and annual cost analysis

Two of the five common economic comparisons are present worth and annual cost analysis. These two comparisons are very similar despite one being opposite signs or values. In simple terms, present worth analysis looks for the maximum present worth of competing scenarios. Annual cost analysis simply looks for the minimum Equivalent Uniform Analysis Cost (EUAC) and is sometimes referred to as annual return method or the capital recovery method. Both these comparisons use standard discount factors to calculate the present worth or the annual cost of the respective scenarios. Both of these analyses require the projects of interest to be mutually exclusive. Both of these types of analysis are simple to apply to commercial or government projects, although present worth is rarely used for government analysis.

Copyright © Mometrix Media. You have been licensed one copy of this document for personal use only. Any other reproduction or redistribution is strictly prohibited. All rights reserved.

## Centroid of an area

The centroid of an area is the exact center of an area. If a force is distributed evenly over an area, you can replace the distributed force with a single force at the centroid regardless of the geometry of the area. Common examples of the centorid of an area is finding a single point that balances a two dimensional shape or calculating the torque produced by a windmill. For common shapes such as circles, rectangles, and triangles, the centroid of the area can be identified by inspection without calculation. For a combination of regular shapes, you can combine the individual areas times their individual centroids divided by the total area. For irregular shapes, integral calculus is required to determine the centroid, where the reciprocal of the area times the integral is of the Cartesian coordinate times the differential area.

## Resultant forces

The resultant force is an equivalent single force that acts on a body that replaces two or more actual forces. Calculations for acceleration and deformations can use the single resultant force instead of the individual forces. The skill to calculate resultant forces was developed in grade school using number lines. In fact, one dimensional resultant forces are calculated exactly the same as number lines and are simply added using a sign convention of forces in one arbitrary direction as positive and forces in the opposite direction as negative. For two and three dimensional resultant forces, the most common technique is to take break down the forces using sine and cosine trigonometric functions into Cartesian components which can then be added together in each axis and then reconstituted into a single force at a particular direction.

## Charts and tables

Charts and tables are ways of organizing information into separate rows and columns that are labeled to identify and explain the data contained in them. Some charts and tables are organized horizontally, with row lengths giving the details about the labeled information. Other charts and tables are organized vertically, with column heights giving the details about the labeled information.

Frequency Tables show how frequently each unique value appears in the set. A Relative Frequency Table is one that shows the proportions of each unique value compared to the entire set. Relative frequencies are given as percents; however, the total percent for a relative frequency table will not necessarily equal 100 percent due to rounding. An example of a frequency table with relative frequencies is below.

| Favorite Color | Frequency | Relative Frequency |
|---|---|---|
| Blue | 4 | 13% |
| Red | 7 | 22% |
| Purple | 3 | 9% |
| Green | 6 | 19% |
| Cyan | 12 | 38% |

Copyright © Mometrix Media. You have been licensed one copy of this document for personal use only. Any other reproduction or redistribution is strictly prohibited. All rights reserved.

**Graphs**

Pictograph s
A Pictograph is a graph, generally in the horizontal orientation, that uses pictures or symbols to represent the data. Each pictograph must have a key that defines the picture or symbol and gives the quantity each picture or symbol represents. Pictures or symbols on a pictograph are not always shown as whole elements. In this case, the fraction of the picture or symbol shown represents the same fraction of the quantity a whole picture or symbol stands for. For example, a row with $3\frac{1}{2}$ ears of corn, where each ear of corn represents 100 stalks of corn in a field, would equal $3\frac{1}{2} \cdot 100 = 350$ stalks of corn in the field.

Circle graphs
Circle Graphs, also known as *Pie Charts*, provide a visual depiction of the relationship of each type of data compared to the whole set of data. The circle graph is divided into sections by drawing radii to create central angles whose percentage of the circle is equal to the individual data's percentage of the whole set. Each 1% of data is equal to 3.6º in the circle graph. Therefore, data represented by a 90º section of the circle graph makes up 25% of the whole. When complete, a circle graph often looks like a pie cut into uneven wedges. Below is an example of a pie chart.

Line graphs
Line Graphs have one or more lines of varying styles (solid or broken) to show the different values for a set of data. The individual data are represented as ordered pairs, much like on a Cartesian plane. In this case, the *x*- and *y*- axes are defined in terms of their units, such as dollars or time. The individual plotted points are joined by line segments to show whether the value of the data is increasing (line sloping upward), decreasing (line sloping downward) or staying the same (horizontal line). Multiple sets of data can be graphed on the same line graph to give an easy visual comparison. An example of this would be graphing achievement test scores for different groups of students over the same time period to see which group had the greatest increase or decrease in performance from year-to-year.

Line plot or dot plot
A Line Plot, also known as a Dot Plot, has plotted points that are NOT connected by line segments. In this graph, the horizontal axis lists the different possible values for the data, and the vertical axis lists the number of times the individual value occurs. A single dot is graphed for each value to show the number of times it occurs. This graph is more closely related to a bar graph than a line graph. Do not connect the dots in a line plot or it will misrepresent the data.

Stem and leaf plot
A Stem and Leaf Plot is useful for depicting groups of data that fall into a range of values. Each piece of data is separated into two parts: the first, or left, part is called the stem; the second, or right, part is called the leaf. Each stem is listed in a column from smallest to largest. Each leaf that has the common stem is listed in that stem's row from smallest to largest. For example, in a set of two-digit numbers, the digit in the tens place is the stem, and the digit in the ones place is the leaf. With a stem and leaf plot, you can easily see which subset of numbers (10s, 20s, 30s, etc.) is the largest. This information is also readily available by looking at a histogram, but a stem and leaf plot also allows you to look closer and see exactly which values fall in that range. Below is an example of a stem and leaf plot.

Copyright © Mometrix Media. You have been licensed one copy of this document for personal use only. Any other reproduction or redistribution is strictly prohibited. All rights reserved.

| Test Scores | |
|---|---|
| **7** | 4 8 |
| **8** | 2 5 7 8 8 |
| **9** | 0 0 1 2 2 3 5 8 9 |

## Bar graphs

A Bar Graph is one of the few graphs that can be drawn correctly in two different configurations – both horizontally and vertically. A bar graph is similar to a line plot in the way the data is organized on the graph. Both axes must have their categories defined for the graph to be useful. Rather than placing a single dot to mark the point of the data's value, a bar, or thick line, is drawn from zero to the exact value of the data, whether it is a number, percentage, or other numerical value. Longer bar lengths correspond to greater data values. To read a bar graph, read the labels for the axes to find the units being reported. Then look where the bars end in relation to the scale given on the corresponding axis and determine the associated value.

## Histograms

At first glance, a Histogram looks like a vertical bar graph. The difference is that a bar graph has a separate bar for each piece of data and a histogram has one continuous bar for each Range of data. For example, a histogram may have one bar for the range 0–9, one bar for 10–19, etc. While a bar graph has numerical values on one axis, a histogram has numerical values on both axes. Each range is of equal size, and they are ordered left to right from lowest to highest. The height of each column on a histogram represents the number of data values within that range. Like a stem and leaf plot, a histogram makes it easy to glance at the graph and quickly determine which range has the greatest quantity of values. A simple example of a histogram is below.

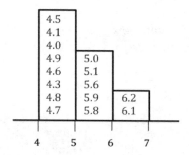

## Bivariate data in a scatter plot

Bivariate Data is simply data from two different variables. (The prefix bi- means two.) In a Scatter Plot, each value in the set of data is plotted on a grid similar to a Cartesian plane, where each axis represents one of the two variables. By looking at the pattern formed by the points on the grid, you can often determine whether or not there is a relationship between the two variables, and what that relationship is, if it exists. The variables may be directly proportionate, inversely proportionate, or show no proportion at all. It may also be possible to determine if the data is linear, and if so, to find an equation to relate the two variables.

Copyright © Mometrix Media. You have been licensed one copy of this document for personal use only. Any other reproduction or redistribution is strictly prohibited. All rights reserved.

## Measures of central tendency

A Measure of Central Tendency is a statistical value that gives a general tendency for the center of a group of data. There are several different ways of describing the measure of central tendency. Each one has a unique way it is calculated, and each one gives a slightly different perspective on the data set. Whenever you give a measure of central tendency, always make sure the units are the same. If the data has different units, such as hours, minutes, and seconds, convert all the data to the same unit, and use the same unit in the measure of central tendency. If no units are given in the data, do not give units for the measure of central tendency.

### Mean
The statistical Mean of a group of data is the same as the arithmetic average of that group. To find the mean of a set of data, first convert each value to the same units, if necessary. Then find the sum of all the values, and count the total number of data values, making sure you take into consideration each individual value. If a value appears more than once, count it more than once. Divide the sum of the values by the total number of values and apply the units, if any. Note that the mean does not have to be one of the data values in the set, and may not divide evenly.

$$\text{mean} = \frac{\text{sum of the data values}}{\text{quantity of data values}}$$

While the mean is relatively easy to calculate and averages are understood by most people, the mean can be very misleading if used as the sole measure of central tendency. If the data set has outliers (data values that are unusually high or unusually low compared to the rest of the data values), the mean can be very distorted, especially if the data set has a small number of values. If unusually high values are countered with unusually low values, the mean is not affected as much. For example, if five of twenty students in a class get a 100 on a test, but the other 15 students have an average of 60 on the same test, the class average would appear as 70. Whenever the mean is skewed by outliers, it is always a good idea to include the median as an alternate measure of central tendency.

### Median
The statistical Median is the value in the middle of the set of data. To find the median, list all data values in order from smallest to largest or from largest to smallest. Any value that is repeated in the set must be listed the number of times it appears. If there are an odd number of data values, the median is the value in the middle of the list. If there is an even number of data values, the median is the arithmetic mean of the two middle values.

### Mode
The statistical Mode is the data value that occurs the most number of times in the data set. It is possible to have exactly one mode, more than one mode, or no mode. To find the mode of a set of data, arrange the data like you do to find the median (all values in order, listing all multiples of data values). Count the number of times each value appears in the data set. If all values appear an equal number of times, there is no mode. If one value appears more than any other value, that value is the mode. If two or more values appear the same number of times, but there are other values that appear fewer times and no values that appear more times, all of those values are the modes.

*Copyright © Mometrix Media. You have been licensed one copy of this document for personal use only. Any other reproduction or redistribution is strictly prohibited. All rights reserved.*

<u>Disadvantages of using median or mode as an only measure of central tendency</u>
The main disadvantage of using the median as a measure of central tendency is that is relies solely on a value's relative size as compared to the other values in the set. When the individual values in a set of data are evenly dispersed, the median can be an accurate tool. However, if there is a group of rather large values or a group of rather small values that are not offset by a different group of values, the information that can be inferred from the median may not be accurate because the distribution of values is skewed. The main disadvantage of the mode is that the values of the other data in the set have no bearing on the mode. The mode may be the largest value, the smallest value, or a value anywhere in between in the set. The mode only tells which value or values, if any, occurred the most number of times. It does not give any suggestions about the remaining values in the set.

**Measure of dispersion**

A Measure of Dispersion is a single value that helps to "interpret" the measure of central tendency by providing more information about how the data values in the set are distributed about the measure of central tendency. The measure of dispersion helps to eliminate or reduce the disadvantages of using the mean, median, or mode as a single measure of central tendency, and give a more accurate picture of the data set as a whole. To have a measure of dispersion, you must know or calculate the range, standard deviation, or variance of the data set.

<u>Range</u>
The Range of a set of data is the difference between the greatest and lowest values of the data in the set. To calculate the range, you must first make sure the units for all data values are the same, and then identify the greatest and lowest values. Use the formula range = highest value – lowest value. If there are multiple data values that are equal for the highest or lowest, just use one of the values in the formula. Write the answer with the same units as the data values you used to do the calculations.

<u>Standard deviation</u>
Standard Deviation is a measure of dispersion that compares all the data values in the set to the mean of the set to give a more accurate picture. To find the standard deviation of a population, use the formula:

$$\sigma = \sqrt{\frac{\sum_{i=1}^{n}(x_i - \bar{x})^2}{n}}$$

where $\sigma$ is the standard deviation of a population, $x$ represents the individual values in the data set, $\bar{x}$ is the mean of the data values in the set, and $n$ is the number of data values in the set. The higher the value of the standard deviation is, the greater the variance of the data values from the mean.

<u>Variance</u>
The Variance of a population, or just variance, is the square of the standard deviation of that population. While the mean of a set of data gives the average of the set and gives information about where a specific data value lies in relation to the average, the variance of the population gives information about the degree to which the data values are spread out and tell you how close an individual value is to the average compared to the other values. The units associated with variance are the same as the units of the data values.

Copyright © Mometrix Media. You have been licensed one copy of this document for personal use only. Any other reproduction or redistribution is strictly prohibited. All rights reserved.

## Percentiles and quartiles

Percentiles and Quartiles are other methods of describing data within a set. Percentiles tell what percentage of the data in the set fall below a specific point. For example, achievement test scores are often given in percentiles. A score at the 80th percentile is one which is equal to or higher than 80 percent of the scores in the set. In other words, 80 percent of the scores were lower than that score. Quartiles are percentile groups that make up quarter sections of the data set. The first quartile is the 25th percentile. The second quartile is the 50th percentile; this is also the median of the data set. The third quartile is the 75th percentile.

## 5-number summary and box-and-whiskers plot

The 5-Number Summary of a set of data gives a very informative picture of the set. The five numbers in the summary include the minimum value, maximum value, and the three quartiles. This information gives the reader the range and median of the set, as well as an indication of how the data is spread about the median. A Box-and-Whiskers Plot is a graphical representation of the 5-number summary. To draw a box-and-whiskers plot, plot the points of the 5-number summary on a number line. Draw a box whose ends are through the points for the first and third quartiles. Draw a vertical line in the box through the median to divide the box in half. Draw a line segment from the first quartile point to the minimum value, and from the third quartile point to the maximum value.

## Skewness

Skewness is a way to describe the symmetry or asymmetry of the distribution of values in a data set. If the distribution of values is symmetrical, there is no skew. In general the closer the mean of a data set is to the median of the data set, the less skew there is. Generally, if the mean is to the right of the median, the data set is Positively Skewed, or right-skewed, and if the mean is to the left of the median, the data set is negatively skewed, or left-skewed. However, this rule of thumb is not infallible. When the data values are graphed on a curve, a set with no skew will be a perfect bell curve. To estimate skew, use the formula:

$$\text{skew} = \frac{\sqrt{n(n-1)}}{n-2} \left( \frac{\frac{1}{n}\sum_{i=1}^{n}(x_i - \bar{x})^3}{\left(\frac{1}{n}\sum_{i=1}^{n}(x_i - \bar{x})^2\right)^{\frac{3}{2}}} \right)$$

where n is the number of values is the set, $x_i$ is the ith value in the set, and $\bar{x}$ is the mean of the set.

## Simple regression

In statistics, Simple Regression is using an equation to represent a relation between an independent and dependent variables. The independent variable is also referred to as the explanatory variable or the predictor, and is generally represented by the variable x in the equation. The dependent variable, usually represented by the variable y, is also referred to as the response variable. The equation may be any type of function – linear, quadratic,

Copyright © Mometrix Media. You have been licensed one copy of this document for personal use only. Any other reproduction or redistribution is strictly prohibited. All rights reserved.

exponential, etc. The best way to handle this task is to use the regression feature of your graphing calculator. This will easily give you the curve of best fit and provide you with the coefficients and other information you need to derive an equation.

**Scatter plots**

Scatter plots are useful in determining the type of function represented by the data and finding the simple regression. Linear scatter plots may be positive or negative. Nonlinear scatter plots are generally exponential or quadratic. These are some common types of scatter plots:

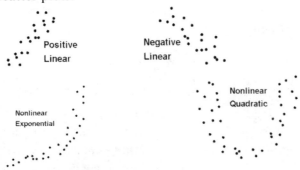

Line of best fit, regression coefficients, residuals, and least-squares regression line
In a scatter plot, the Line of Best Fit is the line that best shows the trends of the data. The line of best fit is given by the equation $\hat{y} = ax + b$, where 'a' and 'b' are the regression coefficients. The regression coefficient 'a' is also the slope of the line of best fit, and 'b' is also the y-coordinate of the point at which the line of best fit crosses the x-axis. Not every point on the scatter plot will be on the line of best fit. The differences between the y-values of the points in the scatter plot and the corresponding y-values according to the equation of the line of best fit are the residuals. The line of best fit is also called the least-squares regression line because it is also the line that has the lowest sum of the squares of the residuals.

**Correlation coefficient**

The Correlation Coefficient is the numerical value that indicates how strong the relationship is between the two variables of a linear regression equation. A correlation coefficient of −1 is a perfect negative correlation. A correlation coefficient of +1 is a perfect positive correlation. Correlation coefficients close to −1 or +1 are very strong correlations. A correlation coefficient equal to zero indicates there is no correlation between the two variables. This test is a good indicator of whether or not the equation for the line of best fit is accurate. The formula for the correlation coefficient is

$$r = \frac{\sum_{i=1}^{n}(x_i - \bar{x})(y_i - \bar{y})}{\sqrt{\sum_{i=1}^{n}(x_i - \bar{x})^2}\sqrt{\sum_{i=1}^{n}(y_i - \bar{y})^2}}$$

where $r$ is the correlation coefficient, $n$ is the number of data values in the set, $(x_i, y_i)$ is a point in the set, and $\bar{x}$ and $\bar{y}$ are the means.

**68-95-99.7 rule**

The 68–95–99.7 Rule describes how a normal distribution of data should appear when compared to the mean. This is also a description of a normal bell curve. According to this

- 12 -

Copyright © Mometrix Media. You have been licensed one copy of this document for personal use only. Any other reproduction or redistribution is strictly prohibited. All rights reserved.

rule, 68 percent of the data values in a normally distributed set should fall within one standard deviation of the mean (34 percent above and 34 percent below the mean), 95 percent of the data values should fall within two standard deviations of the mean (47.5 percent above and 47.5 percent below the mean), and 99.7 percent of the data values should fall within three standard deviations of the mean, again, equally distributed on either side of the mean. This means that only 0.3 percent of all data values should fall more than three standard deviations from the mean. On the graph below, the normal curve is centered on the y-axis. The x-axis labels are how many standard deviations away from the center you are. Therefore, it is easy to see how the 68-95-99.7 rule can apply.

## Z-scores

A Z-score is an indication of how many standard deviations a given value falls from the mean. To calculate a z-score, use the formula $= \frac{x-\mu}{\sigma}$, where $x$ is the data value, $\mu$ is the mean of the data set, and $\sigma$ is the standard deviation of the population. If the z-score is positive, the data value lies above the mean. If the z-score is negative, the data value falls below the mean. These scores are useful in interpreting data such as standardized test scores, where every piece of data in the set has been counted, rather than just a small random sample. In cases where standard deviations are calculated from a random sample of the set, the z-scores will not be as accurate.

## Population and parameter

In statistics, the Population is the entire collection of people, plants, etc., that data can be collected from. For example, a study to determine how well students in the area schools perform on a standardized test would have a population of all the students enrolled in those schools, although a study may include just a small sample of students from each school. A Parameter is a numerical value that gives information about the population, such as the mean, median, mode, or standard deviation. Remember that the symbol for the mean of a population is μ and the symbol for the standard deviation of a population is σ.

## Sample and statistic

A Sample is a portion of the entire population. Where as a parameter helped describe the population, a Statistic is a numerical value that gives information about the sample, such as mean, median, mode, or standard deviation. Keep in mind that the symbols for mean and standard deviation are different when they are referring to a sample rather than the entire population. For a sample, the symbol for mean is x̄ and the symbol for standard deviation is s. The mean and standard deviation of a sample may or may not be identical to that of the entire population due to a sample only being a subset of the population. However, if the sample is random and large enough, statistically significant values can be attained. Samples are generally used when the population is too large to justify including every element or when acquiring data for the entire population is impossible.

## Inferential statistics and sampling distribution

Inferential Statistics is the branch of statistics that uses samples to make predictions about an entire population. This type of statistics is often seen in political polls, where a sample of the population is questioned about a particular topic or politician to gain an understanding

Copyright © Mometrix Media. You have been licensed one copy of this document for personal use only. Any other reproduction or redistribution is strictly prohibited. All rights reserved.

about the attitudes of the entire population of the country. Often, exit polls are conducted on election days using this method. Inferential statistics can have a large margin of error if you do not have a valid sample. Statistical values calculated from various samples of the same size make up the sampling distribution. For example, if several samples of identical size are randomly selected from a large population and then the mean of each sample is calculated, the distribution of values of the means would be a Sampling Distribution.

**Sampling distribution of the mean**

The Sampling Distribution of the Mean is the distribution of the sample mean, $\bar{x}$, derived from random samples of a given size. It has three important characteristics. First, the mean of the sampling distribution of the mean is equal to the mean of the population that was sampled. Second, assuming the standard deviation is non-zero, the standard deviation of the sampling distribution of the mean equals the standard deviation of the sampled population divided by the square root of the sample size. This is sometimes called the standard error. Finally, as the sample size gets larger, the sampling distribution of the mean gets closer to a normal distribution via the Central Limit Theorem.

**Central Limit Theorem**

According to the Central Limit Theorem, regardless of what the original distribution of a sample is, the distribution of the means tends to get closer and closer to a normal distribution as the sample size gets larger and larger (this is necessary because the sample is becoming more all-encompassing of the elements of the population). As the sample size gets larger, the distribution of the sample mean will approach a normal distribution with a mean of the population mean and a variance of the population variance divided by the sample size.

**Survey studies**

A Survey Study is a method of gathering information from a small group in an attempt to gain enough information to make accurate general assumptions about the population. Once a survey study is completed, the results are then put into a summary report. Survey studies are generally in the format of surveys, interviews, or questionnaires as part of an effort to find opinions of a particular group or to find facts about a group. It is important to note that the findings from a survey study are only as accurate as the sample chosen from the population.

**Correlational studies**

Correlational Studies seek to determine how much one variable is affected by changes in a second variable. For example, correlational studies may look for a relationship between the amount of time a student spends studying for a test and the grade that student earned on the test or between student scores on college admissions tests and student grades in college. It is important to note that correlational studies cannot show a cause and effect, but rather can show only that two variables are or are not potentially correlated.

Copyright © Mometrix Media. You have been licensed one copy of this document for personal use only. Any other reproduction or redistribution is strictly prohibited. All rights reserved.

## Experimental studies

Experimental Studies take correlational studies one step farther, in that they attempt to prove or disprove a cause-and-effect relationship. These studies are performed by conducting a series of experiments to test the hypothesis. For a study to be scientifically accurate, it must have both an experimental group that receives the specified treatment and a control group that does not get the treatment. This is the type of study pharmaceutical companies do as part of drug trials for new medications. Experimental studies are only valid when proper scientific method has been followed. In other words, the experiment must be well-planned and executed without bias in the testing process, all subjects must be selected at random, and the process of determining which subject is in which of the two groups must also be completely random.

## Observational studies

Observational Studies are the opposite of experimental studies. In observational studies, the tester cannot change or in any way control all of the variables in the test. For example, a study to determine which gender does better in math classes in school is strictly observational. You cannot change a person's gender, and you cannot change the subject being studied. The big downfall of observational studies is that you have no way of proving a cause-and-effect relationship because you cannot control outside influences. Events outside of school can influence a student's performance in school, and observational studies cannot take that into consideration.

## Samples

A sample is a piece of the entire population that is selected for a particular study in an effort to gain knowledge or information about the entire population. For most studies, a Random Sample is necessary to produce valid results. Random samples should not have any particular influence to cause sampled subjects to behave one way or another. The goal is for the random sample to be a Representative Sample, or a sample whose characteristics give an accurate picture of the characteristics of the entire population. To accomplish this, you must make sure you have a proper Sample Size, or an appropriate number of elements in the sample.

## Bias and extraneous variables

In statistical studies, biases must be avoided. Bias is an error that causes the study to favor one set of results over another. For example, if a survey to determine how the country views the president's job performance only speaks to registered voters in the president's party, the results will be skewed because a disproportionately large number of responders would tend to show approval, while a disproportionately large number of people in the opposite party would tend to express disapproval. Extraneous Variables are, as the name implies, outside influences that can affect the outcome of a study. They are not always avoidable, but could trigger bias in the result.

## Shapes of frequency curves

The five general shapes of frequency curves are Symmetrical, U-shaped, Skewed, J-shaped, and Multimodal. Symmetrical curves are also known as bell curves or normal curves.

Copyright © Mometrix Media. You have been licensed one copy of this document for personal use only. Any other reproduction or redistribution is strictly prohibited. All rights reserved.

Values equidistant from the median have equal frequencies. U-shaped curves have two maxima – one at each end. Skewed curves have the maximum point off-center. Curves that are negative skewed, or left skewed, have the maximum on the right side of the graph so there is longer tail and lower slope on the left side. The opposite is true for curves that are positive skewed, or right skewed. J-shaped curves have a maximum at one end and a minimum at the other end. Multimodal curves have multiple maxima. For example, if the curve has exactly two maxima, it is called a bimodal curve.

## Sample space and outcome

The total number of all possible results of a random test or experiment is called a sample space, or sometimes a universal sample space. The sample space, represented by one of the variables S, Ω, or U (for universal sample space) has individual elements called outcomes. Other terms for outcome that may be used interchangeably include elementary outcome, simple event, or sample point. The number of outcomes in a given sample space could be infinite or finite, and some tests may yield multiple unique sample sets. For example, tests conducted by drawing playing cards from a standard deck would have one sample space of the card values, another sample space of the card suits, and a third sample space of suit-denomination combinations. Note that on this test, all sample spaces are considered finite.

## Event

An event, represented by the variable E, is a portion of a sample space. It may be one outcome or a group of outcomes from the same sample space. If an event occurs, then the test or experiment will generate an outcome that satisfies the requirement of that event. For example, given a standard deck of 52 playing cards as the sample space, and defining the event as the collection of face cards, then the event will occur if the card drawn is a J, Q, or K. If any other card is drawn, the event is said to have not occurred.

## Probability

Probability is a branch of statistics that deals with the likelihood of something taking place. One classic example is a coin toss. There are only two possible results: heads or tails. The likelihood, or probability, that the coin will land as heads is 1 out of 2 (1/2, 0.5, 50%). Tails has the same probability. Another common example is a 6-sided die roll. The probability of any given number coming up is 1 out of 6.

## Probability measure

For every sample space, each possible outcome has a specific likelihood, or probability, that it will occur. The probability measure, also called the distribution, is a function that assigns a real number probability, from zero to one, to each outcome. For a probability measure to be accurate, every outcome must have a real number probability measure that is greater than or equal to zero and less than or equal to one. Also, the probability measure of the sample space must equal one, and the probability measure of the union of multiple outcomes must equal the sum of the individual probability measures.

Copyright © Mometrix Media. You have been licensed one copy of this document for personal use only. Any other reproduction or redistribution is strictly prohibited. All rights reserved.

## Probability of an event

Probabilities of events are expressed as real numbers from zero to one. They give a numerical value to the chance that a particular event will occur. The probability of an event occurring is the sum of the probabilities of the individual elements of that event. For example, in a standard deck of 52 playing cards as the sample space and the collection of face cards as the event, the probability of drawing a specific face card is $\frac{1}{52} = 0.019$, but the probability of drawing any one of the twelve face cards is $12(0.019) = 0.228$. Note that rounding of numbers can generate different results. If you multiplied 12 by the fraction $\frac{1}{52}$ before converting to a decimal, you would get the answer $\frac{12}{52} = 0.231$.

## Likelihood of outcomes

The likelihood or probability of an outcome occurring, is given by the formula
$$P(E) = \frac{\text{Number of acceptable outcomes}}{\text{Number of possible outcomes}}$$
where $P(E)$ is the probability of an event $E$ occurring, and each outcome is just as likely to occur as any other outcome. If each outcome has the same probability of occurring as every other possible outcome, the outcomes are said to be equally likely to occur. The total number of possible outcomes in the event must be less than or equal to the total number of possible outcomes in the sample space. If the two are equal, then the event is certain to occur and the probability is 1. If the number of outcomes that satisfy the event is zero, then the event is impossible and the probability is 0.

## Determining the outcome

### In a simple sample space
For a simple sample space, possible outcomes may be determined by using a tree diagram or an organized chart. In either case, you can easily draw or list out the possible outcomes. For example, to determine all the possible ways three objects can be ordered, you can draw a tree diagram:

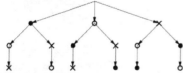

You can also make a chart to list all the possibilities:

| First object | Second object | Third object |
|---|---|---|
| • | X | O |
| • | O | X |
| O | • | X |
| O | X | • |
| X | • | O |
| X | O | • |

Either way, you can easily see there are six possible ways the three objects can be ordered.

### In a less straightforward sample space
When the test on a given sample space does not lend itself to a tree diagram or organized chart, you can use other methods, such as the multiplication principle, permutations, or

- 17 -

Copyright © Mometrix Media. You have been licensed one copy of this document for personal use only. Any other reproduction or redistribution is strictly prohibited. All rights reserved.

combinations, to determine the total number of possible outcomes. Each of these may also be used for simple sample spaces as well, although tree diagrams or charts may be faster in those situations. The multiplication rule states that the probability of two outcomes occurring simultaneously is the product of their individual probabilities. Permutations are outcomes in which each element must occur in a specific order. Combinations are outcomes in which the elements may be arranged in any order.

## Permutation and combination to calculate the number of outcomes

When trying to calculate the probability of an event using the $\frac{desired\ outcomes}{total\ outcomes}$ formula, you may frequently find that there are too many outcomes to individually count them. Permutation and combination formulas offer a shortcut to counting outcomes. A permutation is an arrangement of a specific number of a set of objects in a specific order. The number of permutations of $r$ items given a set of $n$ items can be calculated as $_nP_r = \frac{n!}{(n-r)!}$. Combinations are similar to permutations, except there are no restrictions regarding the order of the elements. While ABC is considered a different permutation than BCA, ABC and BCA are considered the same combination. The number of combinations of $r$ items given a set of $n$ items can be calculated as $_nC_r = \frac{n!}{r!(n-r)!}$ or $_nC_r = \frac{_nP_r}{r!}$.

Example: Suppose you want to calculate how many different 5-card hands can be drawn from a deck of 52 cards. This is a combination since the order of the cards in a hand does not matter. There are 52 cards available, and 5 to be selected. Thus, the number of different hands is $_{52}C_5 = \frac{52!}{5! \times 47!} = 2,598,960$.

## Random variable and probability distribution

In probability, the random variable is not really a variable, but rather a function that generates a variable with a real number value that is determined purely by chance and assigned to each possible outcome of a sample space. Once the values of the random variable have been determined, a probability distribution is set up. The probability distribution can be a chart, graph, formula, or table that gives the individual probabilities of all the values of the random variable. It described the range of possibilities for the random variable, and gives the probability of the random variable falling somewhere within that range.

## Complement of an event

Sometimes it may be easier to calculate the possibility of something not happening, or the complement of an event. Represented by the symbol $\bar{A}$, the complement of A is the probability that event A does not happen. When you know the probability of event A occurring, you can use the formula $P(\bar{A}) = 1 - P(A)$, where $P(\bar{A})$ is the probability of event $A$ not occurring, and $P(A)$ is the probability of event $A$ occurring.

## Addition rule for probability

The addition rule for probability is used for finding the probability of a compound event. Use the formula $P(A \text{ or } B) = P(A) + P(B) - P(A \text{ and } B)$, where $P(A \text{ and } B)$ is the probability of both events occurring to find the probability of a compound event. The

Copyright © Mometrix Media. You have been licensed one copy of this document for personal use only. Any other reproduction or redistribution is strictly prohibited. All rights reserved.

probability of both events occurring at the same time must be subtracted to eliminate any overlap in the first two probabilities.

## Multiplication rule for probability

The multiplication rule can be used to find the probability of two independent events occurring using the formula $P(A \text{ and } B) = P(A) \times P(B)$, where $P(A \text{ and } B)$ is the probability of two independent events occurring, $P(A)$ is the probability of the first event occurring, and $P(B)$ is the probability of the second event occurring. The multiplication rule can also be used to find the probability of two dependent events occurring using the formula $P(A \text{ and } B) = P(A) \times P(B|A)$, where $P(A \text{ and } B)$ is the probability of two dependent events occurring and $P(B|A)$ is the probability of the second event occurring after the first event has already occurred. Before using the multiplication rule, you MUST first determine whether the two events are dependent or independent.

## Mutually exclusive, independent, and dependent

If two events have no outcomes in common, they are said to be mutually exclusive. For example, in a standard deck of 52 playing cards, the event of all card suits is mutually exclusive to the event of all card values. If two events have no bearing on each other so that one event occurring has no influence on the probability of another event occurring, the two events are said to be independent. For example, rolling a standard six-sided die multiple times does not change that probability that a particular number will be rolled from one roll to the next. If the outcome of one event does affect the probability of the second event, the two events are said to be dependent. For example, if cards are drawn from a deck, the probability of drawing an ace after an ace has been drawn is different than the probability of drawing an ace if no ace (or no other card, for that matter) has been drawn.

## Conditional probability

Conditional probability is the probability of an event occurring once another event has already occurred. Given event $A$ and dependent event $B$, the probability of event $B$ occurring when event $A$ has already occurred is represented by the notation $P(A|B)$. To find the probability of event $B$ occurring, take into account the fact that event $A$ has already occurred and adjust the total number of possible outcomes. For example, suppose you have ten balls numbered 1–10 and you want ball number 7 to be pulled in two pulls. On the first pull, the probability of getting the 7 is $\frac{1}{10}$ because there is one ball with a 7 on it and 10 balls to choose from. Assuming the first pull did not yield a 7, the probability of pulling a 7 on the second pull is now $\frac{1}{9}$ because there are only 9 balls remaining for the second pull.

## Probability that at least one of something will occur

Use a combination of the multiplication rule and the rule of complements to find the probability that at least one outcome of the element will occur. This given by the general formula $P(\text{at least one event occurring}) = 1 - P(\text{no outcomes occurring})$. For example, to find the probability that at least one even number will show when a pair of dice is rolled, find the probability that two odd numbers will be rolled (no even numbers) and subtract from one. You can always use a tree diagram or make a chart to list the possible outcomes

Copyright © Mometrix Media. You have been licensed one copy of this document for personal use only. Any other reproduction or redistribution is strictly prohibited. All rights reserved.

when the sample space is small, such as in the dice-rolling example, but in most cases it will be much faster to use the multiplication and complement formulas.

## Odds in favor

In probability, the odds in favor of an event are the number of times the event will occur compared to the number of times the event will not occur. To calculate the odds in favor of an event, use the formula $\frac{P(A)}{1-P(A)}$, where $P(A)$ is the probability that the event will occur. Many times, odds in favor is given as a ratio in the form $\frac{a}{b}$ or $a{:}b$, where $a$ is the probability of the event occurring and $b$ is the complement of the event, the probability of the event not occurring. If the odds in favor are given as 2:5, that means that you can expect the event to occur two times for every 5 times that it does not occur. In other words, the probability that the event will occur is $\frac{2}{2+5} = \frac{2}{7}$.

## Odds against

In probability, the odds against an event are the number of times the event will not occur compared to the number of times the event will occur. To calculate the odds against an event, use the formula $\frac{1-P(A)}{P(A)}$, where $P(A)$ is the probability that the event will occur. Many times, odds against is given as a ratio in the form $\frac{b}{a}$ or $b{:}a$, where $b$ is the probability the event will not occur (the complement of the event) and $a$ is the probability the event will occur. If the odds against an event are given as 3:1, that means that you can expect the event to not occur 3 times for every one time it does occur. In other words, 3 out of every 4 trials will fail.

## Expected value

Expected value is a method of determining expected outcome in a random situation. It is really a sum of the weighted probabilities of the possible outcomes. Multiply the probability of an event occurring by the weight assigned to that probability (such as the amount of money won or lost). A practical application of the expected value is to determine whether a game of chance is really fair. If the sum of the weighted probabilities is greater than or equal to zero, the game is generally considered fair because the player has a fair chance to win, or at least to break even. If the expected value is less than one, then players lose more than they win. For example, a lottery drawing allows the player to choose any three-digit number, 000–999. The probability of choosing the winning number is 1:1000. If it costs $1 to play, and a winning number receives $500, the expected value is $\left(-\$1 \cdot \frac{999}{1{,}000}\right) + \left(\$500 \cdot \frac{1}{1{,}000}\right) = -0.499$ or $-\$0.50$. You can expect to lose on average 50 cents for every dollar you spend.

## Empirical probability

Empirical probability is based on conducting numerous repeated experiments and observations rather than by applying pre-defined formulas to determine the probability of an event occurring. To find the empirical probability of an event, conduct repeated trials (repetitions of the same experiment) and record your results. The empirical probability of

Copyright © Mometrix Media. You have been licensed one copy of this document for personal use only. Any other reproduction or redistribution is strictly prohibited. All rights reserved.

an event occurring is the number of times the event occurred in the experiment divided by the total number of trials you conducted to get the number of events. Notice that the total number of trials is used, not the number of unsuccessful trials. A practical application of empirical probability is the insurance industry. There are no set functions that define life span, health, or safety. Insurance companies look at factors from hundreds of thousands of individuals to find patterns that they then use to set the formulas for insurance premiums.

### Objective probability and subjective probability

Objective probability is based on mathematical formulas and documented evidence. Examples of objective probability include raffles or lottery drawings where there is a pre-determined number of possible outcomes and a predetermined number of outcomes that correspond to an event. Other cases of objective probability include probabilities of rolling dice, flipping coins, or drawing cards. Most gambling is based on objective probability. Subjective probability is based on personal or professional feelings and judgments. Often, there is a lot of guesswork following extensive research. Areas where subjective probability is applicable include sales trends and business expenses. Attractions set admission prices based on subjective probabilities of attendance based on varying admission rates in an effort to maximize their profit.

### Fundamental Counting Principle

The Fundamental Counting Principle deals specifically with situations in which the order that something happens affects the outcome. Specifically, the Fundamental Counting Principle states that if one event can have $x$ possible different outcomes, and after the first outcome has been established the event can then have $y$ possible outcomes, then there are $x \cdot y$ possible different ways the outcomes can happen in that order. For example, if two dice are rolled, one at a time, there are 6 possible outcomes for the first die, and 6 possible outcomes for the second die, for a total of $6 \cdot 6 = 36$ total possible outcomes. Also, suppose you have a bag containing one each of a penny, nickel, dime, quarter, and half dollar. There are 5 different possible outcomes the first time you pull a coin. Without replacing the first coin, there are 4 different possible outcomes for the second coin. This makes $5 \cdot 4 = 20$ different possible outcomes for the first two coins drawn when the order the coins are drawn makes a difference.

### Addition Principle

The Addition Principle addresses situations in which two different tasks are completed at separate times with separate outcomes. The Addition Principle states that if one event can have $x$ possible different outcomes, and a second unrelated event can have $y$ possible different outcomes, and none of the outcomes are common to both events, then the total number of possible outcomes for the two separate events occurring at two separate times is $x + y$. If the two events can occur at the same time and some of the outcomes are common to both events, the total number of possible outcomes for the two events is $x + y -$ the number of outcomes common to both events.

### Lagging indicator

Lagging indicators in occupational health and safety are those metrics that have happened after the fact, or after a workplace injury has occurred. They are a useful indicator of the

Copyright © Mometrix Media. You have been licensed one copy of this document for personal use only. Any other reproduction or redistribution is strictly prohibited. All rights reserved.

effects of incidents and can be managed, but they do not provide a proactive opportunity for improvement. Examples of lagging indicators are the number of lost workdays, the number of days an employee is on restricted duty, the cost incurred for medical visits, and the number of recordable injuries. While it is essential to track lagging indicators and target improved performance over time, they do not provide a snapshot of future performance. Lagging indicators are often used to assess actual regulatory compliance and are essential for reporting purposes.

### Leading indicator

A leading indicator is an objective measure that is used to assess actions taken proactively to improve organizational performance. This is a useful measure in evaluating the impact of an occupational health and safety management system because it measures what the organization is doing to prevent injuries and improve effectiveness in a proactive manner instead of reacting to incidents. Examples of leading indicators are: the number of training courses given, the number of safety meetings held, the number of behavioral safety observations completed, the number of area safety inspections completed, and the number of near miss root cause analyses completed. These leading indicators can be used to assess overall proactive performance, and thorough implementation of the leading indicator activities can strengthen the occupational health and safety program.

### Near miss reporting

A near miss is an incident that comes very close to being an occupational injury but does not result in injury. Examples include having something fall off a highly stacked pallet of material and nearly hit a worker standing nearby, or two forklifts backing up toward each other and nearly crashing in to each other, or an employee using a box cutter that slips and cuts his glove but misses cutting his hand. Diligent monitoring of near misses and responding to them as if they were injury incidents by completing root cause analyses and developing action plans to prevent recurrences can put into place the systems, procedures, and practices that create a safe work environment that responds to incidents before they occur.

### Inspection frequency and response

Routinely scheduled inspections are an integral part of an effective occupational health and safety system. The frequency of inspections must be aligned with the degree of risk posed by the operation, in conjunction with regulatory requirements. Inspections that are conducted too infrequently are a sign of a lax occupational health and safety management system that potentially allows noncompliance or nonconformance to exist without correction between inspections. Moreover, the timeliness and attention paid to correcting issues identified in inspections is an indicator of the effectiveness of the health and safety system. Companies that recognize the importance of timely corrective action will realize the benefits of maintaining a safe work environment that promptly responds to issues identified.

### Calculating incidence rates

The Total Case Incident Rate (TCIR) is a health and safety metric that calculates the total number of OSHA recordable injury cases in a year and is weighted by the number of total

Copyright © Mometrix Media. You have been licensed one copy of this document for personal use only. Any other reproduction or redistribution is strictly prohibited. All rights reserved.

hours worked by employees at the organization during the year to allow comparison between companies in similar industries. The formula to calculate the TCIR is as follows: TCIR = (Number of recordable injuries in calendar year x 200,000) ÷ (Total hours worked) The Days Away, Restricted Duty, or Transfer (DART) is a measure of the number of injury cases that involved days off work, on restricted duty, or transferred to another job. Note that the calculation uses the number of cases, not the total number of days. The calculation is as follows:

DART = (Number of cases with days away, job restriction, or transfer x 200,000) ÷ (Total hours worked)

Ideally, the DART is lower than the TCIR. The 200,000 hours figure refers to the number of hours worked in a year by a company with 100 full-time employees.

**Direct costs of incidents**

The direct costs of an incident are actual monetary costs attributable to the incident. In the case of an injury, the direct costs are the medical bills for the treatment of the injured worker, the money paid to a worker as worker's compensation payments during lost work time, the cost of medications, and the cost of transportation to and from the clinic to attend doctors' appointments. These costs can be readily identified by collecting the invoices from these various services and totaling them. However, in the case of an injury, the direct costs are usually borne by the insurance company and are not readily apparent to the organization.

**Economic and noneconomic costs of an incident**

Economic
The economic costs of an accident or occupational injury include more than the cost for medical treatment of the injured worker. Additional economic costs to consider include the future impact on the worker's compensation costs, the productivity loss represented by a worker that cannot do 100 percent of his duties, the actual lost wages due to the temporary disability benefits not replacing all of the employee's wages, and the cost of replacing that worker on a temporary basis with either other workers' overtime or hiring a replacement. Also contributing to the economic cost of an incident is the staff time that must be devoted to managing the worker's compensation claim, investigating the incident, and putting into place a corrective action plan. Totaling these costs quickly makes it apparent that the economic costs of an incident are broad and are immediately detrimental to the bottom line.

Noneconomic
There are noneconomic costs to occupational injuries that can be quite detrimental to an organization. There is the effect of an incident on the morale of the injured worker, especially if the injured worker perceives that management did not take the unsafe situation that contributed to his injury seriously. This effect on morale can easily extend to others in the workplace that have not been injured. Additional noneconomic costs include the potential for employee absenteeism when the workplace is viewed as high hazard. Poor morale caused by incidents may also contribute to poor productivity. Although these noneconomic costs are not often directly measurable, they do translate into economic costs over the long run and must be managed carefully to prevent them from spiraling out of control.

Copyright © Mometrix Media. You have been licensed one copy of this document for personal use only. Any other reproduction or redistribution is strictly prohibited. All rights reserved.

## Effects on company profitability

Both economic and noneconomic costs of incidents can adversely affect company profitability. The company with a high incident rate is forced to pay more for many of the human factors associated with production. They will have to recruit and train more employees to replace those lost to attrition and voluntary turnover, they will have to pay more for worker's compensation insurance, and will pay more for staff to manage the training programs and return to work programs. In extreme cases, word of a high incident rate can leak into the marketplace and damage a company's overall reputation, leading to reduced sales of the company's product. All of these costs can have a directly adverse effect on company profitability.

Copyright © Mometrix Media. You have been licensed one copy of this document for personal use only. Any other reproduction or redistribution is strictly prohibited. All rights reserved.

# Measuring, Evaluating, and Controlling Hazards

## Negligence, willful/reckless conduct, liability, and care

Negligence is defined as failing to take reasonable care to prevent harm to humans or property damage. It can be further defined as:
- Gross negligence – intentional neglect of duties.
- Contributory negligence – when the injured person contributed to the accident in some way.
- Comparative negligence – determines the negligence of each person involved in an accident.

Willful/reckless conduct is a step beyond gross negligence and occurs when someone intentionally neglects his or her responsibility for reasonable care.
Liability refers to a legal obligation to pay for an act or omission that caused some form of injury, whether physical, financial, or emotional. Strict liability means that a company must pay for damages caused by a product they produced, regardless of fault.
Care is the opposite of negligence and refers to taking steps to ensure that people aren't harmed or property damaged. Types of care include the following:
- Reasonable care – amount of care a prudent person would take
- Great care – amount of care an extra prudent person would take
- Slight care – care less than what a prudent person would take
- A related concept is exercise of due care, which states that people have a legal obligation to exercise care.

## Workers' compensation laws

Workers' compensation laws protect workers who are injured on the job. These laws provide payment for lost wages, medical expenses, burial expenses, rehabilitation, and impairments. The laws have six primary objectives:
- To replace the income a worker misses by being unable to work and to provide prompt medical treatment.
- To save workers and employers the time, trouble, and expense of litigation.
- To keep injured workers from turning to public and private charities.
- To encourage employers to develop procedures that prevent and reduce accidents.
- To provide workers with rehabilitation so that they can return to work more quickly.
- To encourage accident investigations not in order to find fault but to prevent similar events from occurring again.

## Importance of safety

First of all, safety is important for a humanitarian reason. We have a moral responsibility to keep employees, co-workers, customers, and society in general safe. Second, safety is important for a legal reason. We are obliged by laws and regulations to meet certain safety standards. These laws and regulations are necessary because different people have different definitions and standards for safety. The laws and regulations provide common standards

Copyright © Mometrix Media. You have been licensed one copy of this document for personal use only. Any other reproduction or redistribution is strictly prohibited. All rights reserved.

for everyone to follow. Third, safety is important for a cost reason, including both the cost of human life and property. Cost calculations need to include money spent paying for both of the following:

- The negative consequences of poor safety (such as injuries and damaged equipment).
- Preventive measures to minimize safety problems.

## Three Es of safety

The three Es of safety are engineering, education, and enforcement. These are three elements that should be part of any safety program.
Engineering refers to changes in processes and procedures, such as the following:

- Using fewer hazardous materials.
- Requiring the use of personal protective equipment.
- Installing systems with warning and fail-safe devices.

Education is a vital part of safety programs. After all, such items as personal protective equipment won't protect anyone if not used properly. Education should include the following:

- Training workers to use tools and equipment safely.
- Educating workers about the hazards of their jobs.
- Training workers about basic safety policies and procedures.

Enforcement means imposed compliance with rules, laws, and regulations – whether company rules or local, state, or Federal laws or regulations. A fourth "E", Enthusiasm, is sometimes added. Enthusiasm refers to encouragement and motivation of people to support safety programs.

## Reducing workers' compensation claims with safety programs

Workers' compensation claims pay workers for injuries they receive due to on-the-job accidents. Therefore, any programs that reduce the frequency and severity of accidents will likewise reduce workers' compensation claims. Some specific strategies safety programs can use include the following:

- Dealing with the fears and stresses that workers and their families feel after an accident.
- Building worker confidence.
- Helping workers rebuild their strength and endurance.
- Helping workers develop new job skills.
- Helping supervisors deal with the paperwork, investigation, and other fallout from the accident.
- Helping supervisors make any necessary job modifications so the injured employee can return to work more quickly.
- Helping co-workers deal with any negative feelings they have toward the injured worker.
- Including management and labor on safety committees in order to foster cooperation and teamwork.
- Providing rewards to teams that meet safety goals.

Copyright © Mometrix Media. You have been licensed one copy of this document for personal use only. Any other reproduction or redistribution is strictly prohibited. All rights reserved.

**Safety, risk, hazard, hazard control, prevention, safety engineering, and safety practices**

Safety means freedom from danger, injury, or risk. Risk is the possibility of suffering harm or loss. Risk can be measured in two ways:
- The likelihood that a dangerous situation will occur.
- The likely severity of the dangerous situation.

A hazard is a dangerous or unsafe condition or activity that can lead to injury, illness, or property damage. Hazard control means the reduction or elimination of a dangerous situation. Prevention means the recognition of hazards and the taking of steps to prevent the hazards from happening. Safety engineering is the use of engineering principles and practices to try to control and minimize hazards and risks in order to increase safety. Safety practices are processes and procedures used to recognize, evaluate, and manage hazards and risks with an ultimate goal of increasing safety.

**Heinrich's Axioms of Industrial Safety**

Heinrich's ten axioms of industrial safety are as follows:
1. Injuries are the result of a completed series of factors, including the accident that caused the injury.
2. Accidents occur because of a person's unsafe act and/or a mechanical or physical hazard.
3. Most accidents are caused by people's unsafe behavior.
4. Unsafe acts and conditions don't always immediately result in an accident.
5. Knowing why people commit unsafe acts can help determine corrective actions.
6. Most accidents are preventable.
7. Accident prevention techniques work hand in hand with quality and productivity techniques.
8. Safety should be a management responsibility because management can ensure the best results.
9. Supervisors play a key role in preventing industrial accidents.
10. Both direct and indirect costs result from accidents.

**Petersen's accident/incident theory**

The accident/incident theory is an outgrowth of the human factors theory. It includes additional elements such as those listed below:
- Ergonomic traps.
- Decision to err.
- Systems failure.

According to the theory, ergonomic traps (such as workstations that are the wrong size) and a conscious or unconscious decision to err combine with overload to lead to human error, which in turn can lead to an accident. Systems failure becomes a factor when systems that could mitigate the human error and prevent an accident fail. These systems can include policies, procedures, training, and inspections.

Copyright © Mometrix Media. You have been licensed one copy of this document for personal use only. Any other reproduction or redistribution is strictly prohibited. All rights reserved.

## Accident prevention

<u>Reactive and proactive approaches</u>
A reactive approach to accident prevention has four basic steps:
1. The accident occurs.
2. An investigation takes place.
3. Results from the investigation are analyzed.
4. Preventive measures are put into place to prevent the accident from happening again.

In this approach, an accident must occur first before preventive measures are put into place. A proactive approach to accident prevention tries to keep accidents from occurring in the first place. This approach has two steps:
1. Analyze potential accidents.
2. Put preventive measures into place to prevent the accidents from occurring.

Both approaches rely on concepts of frequency, severity, and cost to set priorities:
- A frequency strategy focuses on reducing the accidents that occur most frequently.
- A severity strategy focuses on reducing the accidents that cause the most serious injuries or most damage.
- A cost strategy focuses on reducing the accidents that are the most expensive.

<u>Errors in Management System theory</u>
Juran and Demmin developed the Errors in Management Systems theory as a way to show the relationship between management and safety. They define an accident as a type of error that interrupts the normal process of work. They further theorize that most errors – as many as 85% – result from poor processes and procedures developed by management. Workers are simply following the processes they have been given and therefore cannot avoid making and repeating the error. According to this theory, safety programs should focus on improving processes in order to reduce or eliminate errors. Ideally, management and workers should work together to develop safe and productive processes.

<u>Multiple Factor Theory and Energy Theory</u>
The Multiple Factor Theory postulates that accidents are generally caused by many factors working together. The factors change from one incident to another but can generally be classified as one of the four Ms defined by Grose:
- Man (age, skill level, strength, emotional state, etc.).
- Machine (equipment and vehicles, including construction materials, placement of controls, energy sources, etc.).
- Media (environment, road conditions, and weather, such as pollution, snow on the road, fresh vs. salt water, etc.).
- Management (organizational structure, policies, procedures, etc.).

By examining the relationships among these factors, one can analyze processes and procedures and identify ways to prevent or reduce accidents.
Haddon proposed the Energy Theory, which postulates that accidents and injuries often involve energy transfer. Motor vehicle accidents are an example of this type of accident. The theory further states that the severity of injuries is related to the following:
- The amount of energy transferred.

Copyright © Mometrix Media. You have been licensed one copy of this document for personal use only. Any other reproduction or redistribution is strictly prohibited. All rights reserved.

- The way the energy is transferred.
- The speed at which the energy is transferred.

<u>Domino Theory</u>
According to the Domino Theory developed by Heinrich, the sequence of events in an accident can be compared to a series of five dominoes:
1. A social environment that fosters…
2. Undesirable traits such as carelessness, violence, or unsafe habits, leading to an…
3. Unsafe act or condition, which causes an…
4. Incident, which leads to an…
5. Injury

According to this theory, removing any of the earlier dominoes can prevent an injury. The theory especially emphasizes removing the unsafe act or condition: domino number three. The limitation of the domino theory is that it is often too simplistic: many accidents have multiple causes. By relying on the domino theory, a safety program may identify just one primary cause of an incident, ignoring other causes and underlying factors.

**Losses resulting from accidents**

Losses can be to both people and property and include anything related to the accident that costs money. Losses are usually classified as direct or indirect. Direct costs are related directly to an accident and may include the following:
- Cost to replace damaged property, equipment, or materials.
- Cost to repair damage to the environment.
- Fines for any broken laws and regulations.
- Compensation for injured or ill employees who miss work.
- Payment of medical expenses for injured or ill employees.
- Payments made to survivors in case of the death of an employee.
- Costs related to the cleanup or investigation of an accident, including travel and legal services.

Indirect costs are more difficult to determine and may easily be overlooked. They may include the following:
- Lost productivity due to an injured employee's absence from work.
- Lost productivity caused by lower morale.
- Loss of business, orders, and reputation.

**Heinrich's ratios for direct and indirect costs, unsafe acts and unsafe conditions, and incidents/injuries**

Heinrich developed the ratio for direct and indirect costs to convince managers of the importance of preventing accidents. His investigation demonstrated a 4:1 ratio of direct to indirect costs, showing that the final cost of an accident must include more than medical expenses and worker compensation. Heinrich also developed the unsafe acts and unsafe conditions ratio to identify whether accidents are more likely to be caused by unsafe acts versus unsafe conditions. The ratio he developed was 88:10:2 with 88% of accidents caused by unsafe acts, 10% by unsafe conditions, and 2% by unpreventable causes. According to

- 29 -

Copyright © Mometrix Media. You have been licensed one copy of this document for personal use only. Any other reproduction or redistribution is strictly prohibited. All rights reserved.

this ratio, safety programs should focus on employee behavior in order to prevent accidents.

The incident-injury ratio Heinrich developed is 300:29:1. According to this ratio, of every 330 accidents, 300 result in no injuries, 29 cause minor injuries, and one causes a major injury. This ratio demonstrates that an observant manager typically has many opportunities to improve a safety program before a serious accident occurs.

## Estimating cost of accidents

Safety professionals need to be able to determine the cost of accidents in order to prove that accidents are more costly than prevention programs. To estimate the cost of accidents, they need to do the following:

1. Divide accidents into major classes:
   - Those involving lost workdays, permanent partial disabilities, and temporary total disabilities.
   - Those requiring treatment from an outside physician.
   - Those treated with first aid on site, with minimal property damage and work loss time.
   - Those requiring no first aid or physician visits.
2. Examine accounting records to determine the insured costs associated with accidents.
3. Calculate the uninsured costs associated with accidents, including the following:
   - Lost work hours.
   - Medical costs.
   - Property loss and damage.
   - Insurance premiums.
   - Hidden costs such as the cost of the investigation and emergency response.

Once the cost of several accidents over a period of time is known, an estimate can be made of the average cost of an accident in each class.

## Effects of accidents and injuries on the workplace

Workplace accidents and injuries have several negative effects on employees, management, and the company as a whole:
- Financial cost due to fines, medical treatments, death and burial costs, survivor benefits, and safety corrections.
- Lost time from disabling injuries, both from the injury itself and follow-up medical checkups after the injured employee returns to work.
- Damage to employee morale leading to lower productivity.
- Lower productivity while the injured employee is off work.
- Reduced trust in management.
- Increased absenteeism and turnover because employees don't feel safe on the job.

However, accidents and injuries can also have a positive effect of focusing attention on safety issues and accident prevention.

Copyright © Mometrix Media. You have been licensed one copy of this document for personal use only. Any other reproduction or redistribution is strictly prohibited. All rights reserved.

**Anthropometry**

Anthropometry is the science of measuring the human body. Measurements are either static, such as standing height, or dynamic, such as range of motion. Anthropometric data is used in engineering safety to ensure that equipment and tools are adjustable to fit the widest range of sizes whenever possible. For example, office chairs and pallet platforms can often be adjusted for the user's height. Anthropometric data is also used for designing items that cannot be adjusted, such as doorways and control panels. In this case, the principle is to design for the ninety-fifth percentile male when considering size or the fifth percentile female when considering reach. If a ninety-fifth percentile male can fit through a doorway or in a chair, so will smaller people. If a fifth-percentile female can reach a control, taller people will be able to reach it as well.

**Reducing standing hazards**

Standing for long periods of time can cause back pain, sore feet, and varicose veins. To help control this hazard, employers can provide antifatigue mats to provide a cushion between the employees' feet and the hard floor. Antifatigue mats are especially important for employees working on concrete floors. If employees move around from place to place, antifatigue mats will not help. In this case, shoe inserts can provide the same type of cushioning. Employees may need to buy shoes larger than normal in order to accommodate the inserts. Shoes should fit well and allow the toes to move freely. A well-designed workstation can also reduce the hazards of standing. Including a footrest on the workstation allows employees to raise one foot at a time, relieving pressure on the lower back. Adjustable workstations allow employees to set the workstation at a comfortable height.

**Falls**

Effective protection
For effective fall protection, OSHA recommends that companies adhere to the following practices:
- The company should have a written fall protection plan as part of its overall health and safety plan. The plan should include company rules for how and when to use fall protection equipment.
- The company should follow standard fall protection requirements when fall protection equipment must be used, usually when an employee in a general industry is four feet above the floor, when an employee of a construction company is six feet above the ground, or when an employee is on scaffolding 10 feet above the ground.
- The company should provide correct fall protection equipment and ensure that it is not only used, but is used properly.
- The company should inspect, maintain, repair, and replace fall protection equipment regularly.
- The company should provide supervisors and workers with training on how to recognize fall-related hazards and how and when to use fall protection equipment.

Prevention
To prevent people from falling, the following actions should be taken:
- Reduce slipping and tripping hazards.

Copyright © Mometrix Media. You have been licensed one copy of this document for personal use only. Any other reproduction or redistribution is strictly prohibited. All rights reserved.

- Install barriers such as guardrails and covers over holes. OSHA requires that guardrails be at least 42 inches high.
- Install warning devices such as barricades and flags.
- Install handholds for people to use when they are moving up or down ladders or stairs.
- Design doors and walls in multi-story buildings so people cannot fall through them.
- Use railings and shrubs to prevent people from climbing on retaining walls.

In certain situations, such as at construction sites, you may also need to include fall-limiting devices to reduce the possibility of injury if someone does fall. Examples of fall-limiting devices include harnesses, safety nets, and catch platforms.

Fall protection system
A fall protection system can limit or prevent falls. A fall protection system can include safety belts, safety harnesses, lanyards, hardware, grabbing devices, lifelines, fall arrestors, climbing safety systems, and safety nets. Most of these elements stop a fall that has already started and must meet specific standards. Safety belts are worn around the waist while harnesses fit around the chest and shoulders and occasionally the upper legs. Safety harnesses lessen the number and severity of injuries when they arrest a fall because the force is distributed over a larger part of the body. Lanyards and lifelines connect safety harnesses to an anchoring point while grabbing devices connect lanyards to a lifeline. Lanyards absorb energy, so they reduce the impact load on a person when the fall is arrested.

**Anchorage, body belt, body harness, hole, low-slope roof, opening, and positioning device system**

Anchorage is a secure point of attachment for lanyards, lifelines, and deceleration devices. A body belt is a strap secured around the waist and attached to a lanyard, lifeline, or deceleration device. A body harness consists of straps attached to other elements of a personal fall system. In case of a fall, the straps distribute the fall-arrest force over the thighs, pelvis, waist, chest, and shoulders. A hole is defined as any void or gap two inches or larger in a walking or working surface. A low-slope roof is a roof with a slope that is less than or equal to 4 in 12. An opening is any gap or void that is 18 inches or more wide and 30 inches or more high in a wall or partition. A positioning device system is a body belt or body harness that supports a person on a wall so that he or she has both hands free.

**Rigging inspection**

When inspecting rigging, you need to do the following:
- Look for broken outer wires or fibers and any evidence of corrosion, wear, kinking, or crushing.
- Check hooks for cracks.
- Check the jaw opening of the hook to see if it has widened more than 15 degrees, which would indicate it needs to be replaced.
- Check for stiffness between the links on a chain, which suggests that the chain has been overloaded, reducing its load capacity.
- Check that retainers are in place allowing rigging to slip into the jaw but not to slip off.

Copyright © Mometrix Media. You have been licensed one copy of this document for personal use only. Any other reproduction or redistribution is strictly prohibited. All rights reserved.

- Check for damaged segments or links in a chain and for splices in a rope.
- Check the alignment of the fittings.

**Workstation layout**

Workstations need to be designed to make the work as convenient and comfortable as possible so that workers remain safe and productive. Generally, this means placing components where they can be easily seen and reached. Four principles of workstation layout are importance, frequency of use, functionality, and sequence of use.
- Importance – Components that are the most important to the overall system should be the most prominent.
- Frequency of use – Components that are used frequently should be conveniently located.
- Functionality – Components that are functionally related should be grouped together.
- Sequence of use – Components that are operated in sequence should be grouped together and placed in the order they are used.

**Preventing and reducing severity of explosions**

The exact controls used to prevent an explosion or reduce the severity of an explosion will change depending on the materials and use environment. However, some general guidelines include the following:
- Limit the amount of explosive material stored in any one area.
- If large amounts of explosive materials must be stored, they should be in a remote area.
- Regularly clean areas where explosives are stored so dust will not accumulate.
- Eliminate sources of ignition such as lighters, moving belts, and electrical equipment.
- Store fuels and oxidizers in separate locations.
- Install extinguishing and suppression systems to put out fires before an explosion can occur.
- Use vents in any containers where explosive mixtures could lead to explosions.
- Use distance and barriers to separate explosive materials from each other and from populated areas.
- Train anyone handling, using, and distributing explosives.

**Reducing and eliminating heat stress and thermal injuries**

The keys to reducing heat stress and thermal injuries are stated below:
- Control the source by keeping heat sources away from occupied areas.
- Modify the environment through ventilation, shielding, barriers, and air conditioning.
- Adjust activities by making the work easier, limiting time spent in hot environments, and requiring periodic rest breaks.
- Provide protective equipment such as water-cooled and air-cooled clothing, reflective clothing, protective eyewear, gloves, and insulated materials.
- Incorporate physiological and medical examinations and monitoring to identify high-risk people.

Copyright © Mometrix Media. You have been licensed one copy of this document for personal use only. Any other reproduction or redistribution is strictly prohibited. All rights reserved.

- Develop a training program to help workers acclimatize to hot environments and learn safe work habits.

## Controlling structural hazards

Controlling structural hazards requires knowing the technology used in designing, installing, and maintaining the structure. This includes understanding the following:
- Static mechanics and the forces acting on bolts, rivets, welds, chains, and other structural elements.
- Welds.
- Dynamic loading conditions.
- Friction.
- Fluid or hydraulic mechanics.
- Soil, including the moisture content, internal resistance, cohesion, and consolidation.
- Columns.
- Beams.

In addition, controlling structural hazards also requires the following knowledge or actions.
- Knowing how materials behave both when they are new and as they age and understanding the effects of regular use and exposure to radiation, chemicals, and extreme temperatures.
- Making calculations correctly.
- Communicating regularly with other project members, especially when design changes need to be made.
- Analyzing the use environment.
- Assembling the structure carefully.

## Stair safety

The following are terms and safety features related to stair safety:
- Uniformity - Uniformity means that all the steps in a flight of stairs need to have the same dimensions.
- Slip resistance - Slip resistance means that the tread on all the steps in a flight of stairs needs to have the same or very similar slip resistance.
- Slope - Slope refers to the ratio of riser height to tread depth. The slope needs to be the same for all the steps in a stair. The preferred slop is 30-35 degrees.
- Visibility - Visibility means having enough light to see steps and using surface finishes that make the steps easy to see.
- Structure - Structure refers to the anticipated load the steps are designed to carry. According to OSHA regulations, steps must be able to carry five times the live load and at least 1,000 pounds of a moving, concentrated load.
- Width - Width refers to the width of the staircase itself. Stairs in buildings with fewer than 50 occupants must be at least 36 inches wide. Stairs in larger buildings must be at least 44 inches wide.

## Preventing objects from falling on people

To prevent objects from falling on people, the following actions should be taken:

Copyright © Mometrix Media. You have been licensed one copy of this document for personal use only. Any other reproduction or redistribution is strictly prohibited. All rights reserved.

- Follow good housekeeping procedures so that tools and other items are not left on elevated surfaces where they can fall on people below.
- Use guardrails with a toehold and infill so objects cannot fall through the guardrail onto people below.
- Include a restricted fall zone in areas where items are likely to fall. Prevent people from entering the fall zone where they could be struck by falling objects or splattering materials.
- Provide overhead protection and barriers to keep items from assembly lines and conveyer belts from falling on people below.
- Develop and follow safe procedures for stacking and storing materials such as keeping stacks out of aisles and limiting the height of stacks.

## Electrical hazards

Physical controls
Physical controls for electrical hazards include materials, components, and placements. Specific controls include the following:
- Choosing the right wire length is a physical control. Longer wires have more resistance and therefore will heat more.
- Placing electrical equipment where people and other equipment won't come into contact with it is a physical control.
- Using shields and barriers to protect people in areas where electrical lines pass through populated areas is a physical control.
- Using conduits and protective coverings to keep people from touching energized conductors is a physical control.
- Using sealed equipment so sparks and heat do not ignite the surrounding areas is a physical control.
- Using proper connections to keep conductors in close contact with each other is a physical control.
- Using insulation or enclosures to isolate energized portions of electrical equipment from components people can contact is a physical control.

Overcurrent devices limit the amount of current that can flow through a circuit or electrical device. Examples of overcurrent devices include fuses and circuit breakers. Switching devices reduce electrical hazards by preventing access to electrical equipment or interrupting power during dangerous situations. Examples of switching devices include the following:
- Lockouts, which prevent electrical equipment from being turned on.
- Interlocks, which restrict access to energized areas or equipment.
- Cutouts, which interrupt power to electrical equipment if the temperature exceeds a certain level.

Grounding and bonding are both used when there is a difference in charge between two conductors. Bonding equalizes the charge between the two items while grounding removes the charge altogether.

Electrical safety program
NIOSH recommends that an electrical safety program complies with all OSHA regulations and with National Electrical Code and the National Electrical Safety Code. All potential

*Copyright © Mometrix Media. You have been licensed one copy of this document for personal use only. Any other reproduction or redistribution is strictly prohibited. All rights reserved.*

electrical hazards and safety interventions need to be identified during the planning period of maintenance or construction projects. Workers need to receive training on how to identify and control electrical hazards as well as on basic electrical theory, first aid, personal protective equipment, and safe work procedures. Lockout and tagout procedures should also be developed. Personal protective equipment and testing or detection equipment needs to be available. Safety meetings and both scheduled and unscheduled inspections should be conducted regularly.

## Reducing accidents from machines and tools

In addition to guards and devices, the following procedures can help keep operators of tools and machines safe:
- Ensure that everyone operating a machine is trained on how to use the machine, what hazards the machine may pose, and what safeguards the machine has.
- Ensure that workers follow all procedures for using the machine.
- Ensure that all guards and guard devices work correctly.
- Inspect, maintain, and repair machines regularly.
- Ensure that machine operators dress appropriately, with no loose clothing, jewelry, or hair.
- Tag or lockout machines when they are being set up, maintained, or cleaned so they will not be accidentally turned on.

## Power transmission safeguards and point-of-operation safeguards

Power transmission components of a machine transfer power from a motor to moving parts of the machine such as a belt or pulley. To ensure safety, power transmission components need the following safeguards:
- Power transmission guards that enclose hazardous transmission components so people cannot come into contact with them.
- Devices to shut off the machine in case of unauthorized access or emergency situations.
- Warnings on any access points to warn users to cut power to the machine before accessing it.

The point of operation is the location where the machine performs work, such as cutting, punching, or assembling. Point-of-operation guards and devices protect users at this point. Examples of point-of-operation guards include the following:
- Enclosure guards, which keep body parts or clothing from contacting the point of operation.
- Interlocked guards, which keep a machine from operating when a section is open.
- Ring guards, which enclose a rotating cutter.
- Devices keep a machine from operating when an operator's fingers or hands are in the point of operation.

## Controlling noise in the workplace

The primary way to control noise in the workplace is to prevent noise from occurring in the first place by setting noise specification levels for equipment and processes. Where noise can't be avoided, its effects can be reduced by grouping and enclosing noisy processes in a

Copyright © Mometrix Media. You have been licensed one copy of this document for personal use only. Any other reproduction or redistribution is strictly prohibited. All rights reserved.

soundproof area so that people working in other areas are not bothered. Design features that can help reduce noise include the following:

- Controlling the direction of the source.
- Reducing flow rates.
- Reducing driving forces.
- Controlling vibrating surfaces.
- Using barriers and shields.
- Building with sound-absorbing materials.

In addition to controlling the noise source itself, you can also protect the workers by requiring protection such as earplugs or muffs.

## Controlling hazardous chemicals

<u>Appropriate housekeeping, materials handling, leak detection, and training procedures</u>
Part of housekeeping is removing dust and cleaning up spills. Hazardous dust needs to be regularly vacuumed from surfaces so that it will not become airborne. A vacuum that traps the contaminants must be used. Materials can become airborne when they are loaded, unloaded, and transferred to other containers. Transferring within a closed transfer or exhaust system can protect workers from being exposed to airborne dust and vapors. For liquids, it is also helpful to use drip pans or containers to collect overfill spills and leaks. Leak detection programs can include both automatic sensors and regular visual inspections of valves and pipes. The sensors can trigger alarms or even shut down a process. Repairing leaks quickly minimizes any potential exposures. Workers and supervisors who use hazardous chemicals need to receive training on what hazards they face and how to protect themselves. This training will help them stay safe and is also required by OSHA standards and by law in some states.

<u>Work modifications, personal hygiene, and personal protective equipment</u>
One work modification that can help protect workers from chemical hazards involves reducing an individual worker's exposure time to hazardous chemicals during any one work shift. For example, workers can share an activity or task so that each worker remains below the exposure limit. When it comes to chemical hazards, one aspect of personal hygiene refers to cleansing any contaminated skin whether the skin was contaminated during regular work tasks or because of an accident or spill. Procedures should be in place to specify which soaps and cleaners to use for which chemicals. There may also be specific washing stations and showers for different purposes. Hygiene may also include washing eyes that become contaminated as well as safe areas for changing clothes and for eating and drinking. Personal protective equipment provides a final level of protection against chemical hazards. Such equipment may include protective clothing, eyewear, creams and lotions, and respiratory equipment.

<u>Engineering controls</u>
Engineering controls for hazardous chemicals include substitution, isolation, and ventilation:

- Substitution means substituting a non-hazardous or less hazardous material for a hazardous material. For the substitution to be effective, the new material needs to work as effectively as the old material.

Copyright © Mometrix Media. You have been licensed one copy of this document for personal use only. Any other reproduction or redistribution is strictly prohibited. All rights reserved.

- Isolation means creating a barrier between workers and the source of contamination. This barrier could be a glove box that encloses the hazardous material or a separate enclosure that workers can only access remotely. Isolation can also mean separating hazardous and non-hazardous processes.
- Ventilation protects workers from airborne contaminants. With general ventilation, fresh air replaces or dilutes contaminated air. Local exhaust ventilation captures contaminants before they reach people and moves the contaminants to a safe area for treatment.

## Controls for working in confined spaces

Confined spaces include such work areas as tank cars, boilers, silos, underground tunnels, and railroad boxcars. All these spaces have limited entrances and exits and require specific controls to ensure worker safety. Hazards that workers in confined spaces face include toxicity, potential oxygen deficiency, and fire or explosion from flammable or combustible gases or dust. To protect workers, the following actions should be taken:
- Always evaluate a confined space for hazards before workers enter.
- Ensure that the confined space has adequate ventilation.
- Include equipment for suppressing fires and removing smoke and fumes.
- Train workers on safety procedures they need to follow when working in a confined space.
- Institute a buddy system for confined spaces so two workers are always present.

## Grab sample, long-term sample, colorimetry, impinger, centrifugal separator, and electrostatic precipitator

A grab sample is a short-term sample of gas or vapor. A hand pump or squeeze bulb is used to collect the sample. During long-term sampling, air is sampled continuously, typically every 15-30 minutes. This sampling allows the instrumentation to detect if hazardous material has leaked or been released. Examples of long-term sampling equipment include oxygen meters and combustible gas meters. Colorimetry equipment consists of glass tubes containing materials that change color when they react to particular contaminants. These devices let workers know quickly if a contaminant is present. Impingers are a type of filtering device used to capture particulates in air. Other similar types of filtering devices include centrifugal separators and electrostatic precipitators. Centrifugal separators use spinning air to separate particulates from the air. Electrostatic precipitators place a charge on particulates so they will move to an oppositely charged collection plate.

## Air cleaning devices

Air cleaning devices remove contaminants from ventilated air before the air is released outdoors. A mechanical separator removes particles through air velocity. Examples of mechanical separators include gravity chambers and cyclone collectors. Filtration devices separate particles by providing a filter through which the air passes but particulates don't pass. Filters range from low-efficiency mat filters to high-efficiency HEPA filters. Wet collectors trap contaminants in a liquid where it is collected and sometimes cleaned. These types of air cleaning devices are relatively inexpensive, are compact in size, and can handle high temperatures and humidity. Examples of wet collectors include spray chambers, orifice collectors, and packed towers. Electrostatic precipitators place a negative charge on

*Copyright © Mometrix Media. You have been licensed one copy of this document for personal use only. Any other reproduction or redistribution is strictly prohibited. All rights reserved.*

particles as the air passes through. The charged particles then collect on a positively-charged collection plate. Electrostatic precipitators are very efficient but are more expensive than other devices.

## Recirculating air

Once it is cleaned, formerly contaminated air should be recirculated only if it has no potential health consequences for anyone breathing the air. If the air is recirculated, contaminants must be less than the recommended concentrations for health hazards. In addition, the following procedures must be followed:
- The cleaning system must include equally efficient primary and secondary systems or a primary system accompanied by a fail-safe monitor.
- The cleaning system must include a warning system to indicate failures or inefficiencies.
- If a problem occurs, contaminated air must be diverted outside or the process generating the contaminant must be shut down.
- The recirculated air must be tested regularly to ensure that it is safe and that the cleaning system is working properly.

## Ventilation

Ventilation serves many purposes. It keeps flammable gases and vapors and toxic contaminants below dangerous levels. It also provides air movement that can cool workers and help prevent heat stress. Ventilation also reduces odors and helps control microorganisms and dust. Finally, ventilation limits carbon dioxide buildup in closed spaces and tightly sealed buildings. The main types of ventilation are thermal control and general ventilation. Thermal ventilation is designed to change the temperature of an area, usually to cool it but occasionally to warm it. General ventilation, also called dilution ventilation, uses clean air to reduce the level or concentration of contaminants in an area. This type of system is best for processes that generate about the same low level of contaminants every day. For systems that generate large amounts of contaminants or contaminants that are very toxic or flammable, general ventilation may not be able to keep contaminant levels low enough for safety.

## Sick building syndrome

Sick building syndrome occurs when more than 20% of occupants in the same building become ill with symptoms such as headaches, fever, nausea, cough, etc. The symptoms often lessen over the weekend. Sick building syndrome can be linked to poor ventilation, poor lighting and acoustics, and chemical contaminants from furniture and carpeting. To prevent sick building syndrome in existing buildings, contaminants need to be cleaned up and the building needs to be properly maintained. This can include changing dirty air filters, cleaning carpets and furniture, keeping humidity at less than 70 percent, preventing stagnant water from accumulating, and regularly emptying condensate drainage trays. Preventive design in new buildings can make it easier to combat sick building syndrome. Design features should include intake vents that receive fresh air instead of contaminated air and HVAC systems that are easy to inspect and service.

Copyright © Mometrix Media. You have been licensed one copy of this document for personal use only. Any other reproduction or redistribution is strictly prohibited. All rights reserved.

**Hazardous waste**

Hazards and controls
Hazardous waste can be flammable, corrosive, and toxic. In addition, it poses a threat to the environment: it can contaminate water and soil, destroy natural habitats, kill fish, animals, and birds, damage crops, and contribute to air pollution. A key factor to controlling hazardous waste is to eliminate or reduce its production. When possible, processes need to be changed to substitute less hazardous materials or to use materials that don't produce hazardous waste. It is also possible to recycle and reuse some hazardous materials such as solvents. When hazardous materials cannot be eliminated or recycled, they must be safely contained, stored, treated, and disposed of. Containment minimizes contact between the hazardous waste and air, water, soil, and people. Storage may be in tanks, open lagoons, or waste piles. Hazardous materials should always be kept separate from other waste.

Treating and disposing
There are three main methods for treating hazardous waste: biological, chemical, and physical. Biological treatment uses microorganisms such as bacteria to break down organic wastes. Chemical treatment uses acids or bases to adjust the pH of substances in order to extract oils and heavy metals. Physical treatment isolates or concentrates materials through evaporation, adsorption, solidification, cementation, polymerization, or encapsulation. There are two main methods for disposing of hazardous waste: burial and incineration. Hazardous waste can only be buried in secure landfills that meet EPA standards. This is to prevent the waste from leaching into water or surrounding soils. Incineration, or burning, can be a safe form of disposal for many hazardous wastes, excluding heavy metals. Incinerators typically include scrubbers downstream from the combustion process to ensure that contaminated materials don't escape.

**Transporting hazardous materials**

The transporting of hazardous materials poses special threats to life and property. Anyone transporting hazardous materials needs to be familiar with DOT definitions for hazardous materials. To reduce the hazards, DOT regulates the following:
- The type of transportation allowed (For example, radioactive materials cannot be transported on planes, and some hazardous materials cannot be transported on passenger planes or trains).
- The quantity of hazardous material allowed to be shipped at one time.
- Packaging of hazardous materials for transportation.
- Labeling of hazardous materials.
- Transportation routes allowed.
- Shipping papers required.
- Incident reports required.
- Training required of anyone designing packaging, preparing shipments, managing shipments, or driving hazardous materials.

**Storing materials safely**

To store materials safely, the following actions should be taken:
- Use good housekeeping procedures so that everything has a place where it belongs.

Copyright © Mometrix Media. You have been licensed one copy of this document for personal use only. Any other reproduction or redistribution is strictly prohibited. All rights reserved.

- Don't stack materials too high. Stacks that are too high take little force to be knocked over. In addition, if materials are stacked too high, lower boxes can be crushed and the stack could then tip over.
- Use crossties for lumber and bagged materials.
- Use stepping back procedures when materials are stacked in several rows.
- Use retaining walls to restrain bulk materials.
- Use racks to keep items like drums, rolls, and piping from falling.
- Use protective barriers to keep industrial trucks from running into racks.
- Design storage areas with wide enough aisles for industrial trucks if they will later be used to move the stored materials.
- Use netting to catch items that may fall from overhead storage areas.

## Controlling and extinguishing fires

Numerous types of detectors, extinguishers, and alarms are available for controlling and extinguishing fires:
- Heat detectors sense when air temperature becomes too high.
- Smoke detectors use ionization or photoelectricity to sense when smoke is in the air. Smoke detectors usually sense fire before heat detectors do because smoke usually occurs before the heat rises significantly.
- Flame detectors monitor for wavelengths, usually infrared or ultraviolet, that may be thrown off by waves or embers.
- Gas sensors respond to gasses that usually develop during fires.
- Portable extinguishers are available in different types for different classes of fire. They are small enough to be carried and can be used to put out small fires before they spread.
- Water spray smothers fuel and reduces heat.
- Sprinkler systems, whether water-based or chemical-based, are the most effective for controlling fires in large buildings.
- Fire suppression systems based on carbon dioxide, halons, dry chemicals, and foams are useful for extinguishing fires in areas where water would be hazardous, as with electrical fires or flammable liquids.

## Storing flammable and combustible materials indoors

When storing flammable or combustible materials indoors, the following actions should be taken: Store only small amounts in occupied areas or buildings; larger amounts need to be stored in separate facilities. Follow National Fire Protection Association (NFPA) standards when designing storerooms for flammable and combustible materials, including standards for ventilation, static electricity grounding systems, explosion-proof light switches and fixtures, self-closing doors with raised sills, signage, and floor contours. Follow NFPA standards for storage cabinets designed to hold small quantities of flammable and combustible items. When transferring flammables from one container to another, ensure that the containers are touching each other or are connected to a grounding rod or line. Store flammable liquids in closed containers. When dispensing flammable liquids from drums, use gravity or suction pumps rather than pressurizing the drum. Use safety cans to move flammable liquids from their storage area to their point of use. Use plunger cans if you need to wet cleaning cloths with a flammable liquid. Store cloths that have been

- 41 -

Copyright © Mometrix Media. You have been licensed one copy of this document for personal use only. Any other reproduction or redistribution is strictly prohibited. All rights reserved.

contaminated by flammable liquids in a small self-closing container that you empty regularly.

## Building design for improved fire safety

Fire safety in buildings has three goals:
- Getting occupants of the building out safely.
- Keeping property loss as low as possible.
- Reducing interruption of operations.

For optimal fire safety in buildings, building designers should do the following:
- Ensure that fire equipment can get access to all sides of the building without being blocked by landscaping or parking areas.
- Locate water supplies, hydrants, and valves throughout the building.
- Provide enough space between buildings so that fire cannot jump from one building to another.
- Include fire walls, fire resistant doors, dampers, and shutters to confine fire, preventing it from moving to other buildings or other parts of the same building.
- Choose building materials with high fire resistance ratings.

## Product liability

Manufacturers and sellers of a product have a duty to provide their customers with safe products. Product liability is the legal liability manufacturers and sellers face because of injury or damage resulting from the use of their product. Actionable injury or damage could occur for any of the following reasons:
- The product is dangerous or defective.
- The product does not live up to the claims of the manufacturer or seller.
- The manufacturer or seller was negligent.

Product safety can be compromised anytime when a product is being planned, designed, manufactured, marketed, or distributed. Safety engineers can help ensure that companies do the following:
- Follow laws and regulations.
- Anticipate and prevent possible safety problems.
- Detect and remove design defects and include necessary safety features.
- Include appropriate instructions and warnings.
- Anticipate any ways the product could be misused and provide safety features or warnings to mitigate this.

## Ergonomics

Ergonomics is defined as the relationship between people and their environment, including tools, equipment, work area, vehicles, facilities, and printed material. Good ergonomics improves output and performance and reduces error and accidents by making the environment comfortable and user-friendly. The four general principles of ergonomics that apply to safety engineering are as follows:
- People versus machines. This principle states that people are better at some jobs, such as reasoning inductively and handling unexpected occurrences, while

Copyright © Mometrix Media. You have been licensed one copy of this document for personal use only. Any other reproduction or redistribution is strictly prohibited. All rights reserved.

machines are better at other jobs, such as repetitive operations and deductive reasoning.
- Change the job, not the person. People have limits, and not recognizing those limits can cause errors, hazards, and accidents. It is better to change a job, equipment, or environment to fit the person rather than trying to change the person to fit the job.
- Work smart. Productivity can be improved and errors reduce by finding new and better ways to do a job.
- People are different. People differ in their age, height, weight, reaction time, strength, coordination, attitudes, etc. Designers and managers need to adjust jobs accordingly.

Good recordkeeping will help managers determine if their company has an ergonomics problem. Accident reports, first aid logs, and insurance records can all help identify cumulative trauma disorder (CTD) trends. A high rate of specific types of injuries can indicate an ergonomic problem. High rates of employee complaints, absenteeism, or turnover can also indicate ergonomic problems. Second, managers need to observe the workplace, looking for repetitive work, awkward posture, extreme temperatures, manual material handling, high vibration levels, and other hazards that can lead to CTDs. Photographing and videotaping employees while they work can help managers observe and analyze specific tasks. Measuring such factors as how far workers have to carry materials or how high they have to lift something also provides useful information. Managers should also look for changes that employees are making to their workstations. When employees change their workstations to make them more comfortable (such as by adding padding or more light), it may indicate an underlying ergonomic problem.

## Controlling AIDS and bloodborne pathogen hazards

Procedures that can protect workers from AIDS and bloodborne pathogens in the workplace include the following:
- Treating all bodily fluids as if they are contaminated.
- Using self-sheathing needles, leakproof specimen containers, and puncture-proof containers for sharp objects.
- Providing handwashing stations with antiseptic hand cleaners and requiring workers to wash their hands after removing gloves that could be contaminated.
- Prohibiting employees from eating or drinking in areas where bloodborne pathogens could be present.
- Providing gloves, goggles, respirators, aprons, and other personal protective equipment.
- Regularly decontaminating and cleaning equipment and potentially contaminated areas.
- Labeling potential biohazards.

Safety program
An AIDS and bloodborne pathogens policy should be developed before any employees test positive for a disease. Preparing in advance allows the company to spend time determining appropriate actions instead of having to react quickly. An AIDS and bloodborne pathogens policy needs to include at least three elements: employee rights, testing, and education. It should define the rights of employees who have been diagnosed with AIDS or a bloodborne pathogen, including reasonable accommodations that will be made. The policy will also

- 43 -

Copyright © Mometrix Media. You have been licensed one copy of this document for personal use only. Any other reproduction or redistribution is strictly prohibited. All rights reserved.

include whether employees will be tested for AIDS and bloodborne pathogens. Finally, the policy should include procedures for educating workers on how AIDS and other bloodborne pathogens can be transmitted and prevented.

## Reducing workplace stress

Stress can never be completely eliminated from the workplace, but managers can help employees learn to adapt to stress. First, managers can provide training to help employees learn to recognize and deal with stress. They also need to give employees clear and consistent work guidelines, feedback, and as much autonomy as possible. Other methods are to involve employees in decision-making, keep them informed about company changes, and promote teamwork. A safe and pleasant work environment can also help reduce workplace stress. If workloads are too heavy, tasks can be reassigned or redistributed. Training should be provided for all new job assignments. Flexible hours, childcare programs, exercise opportunities, mental health benefits, and other perks can all help reduce workplace stress.

## Reducing risk of workplace violence

Managers can incorporate several strategies into the workplace to prevent or reduce workplace violence. Employers can provide a secure workplace.
- The workplace should be well-lit with no areas that are secluded or isolated.
- Work flows and traffic patterns should be easily observed so employees are never left in a vulnerable position. Employees should have freedom and control within their own area of the workplace but limited access to other areas.
- Surveillance cameras can allow for further monitoring of the workplace.
- Employers can also control access to the workplace. Fencing and locks can restrict trespassers from entering the work area. Security procedures that require visitors to check in reduce the risk of violence from outsiders.
- Managers should seek to provide a positive work environment with clear roles and instructions and positive feedback.
- Employers can adopt procedures to reduce or prevent workplace violence, such as conducting background checks on employees, providing training for dealing with stress, and providing counseling benefits.

## Computer tools used for safety applications

Database management systems help manage safety data, tracking items such as personal protective equipment, training, hazardous materials, and inspections. Modeling helps safety engineers observe the behavior of physical phenomena or people. Modeling is used for such functions as accident reconstruction, gas dispersion, and fires. Computers are useful tools for training, both for providing training through computer-based training and for tracking training hours completed.  Computers are also useful for other kinds of tracking, such as shipments of materials and repair and maintenance activities. Computers are useful as part of monitoring systems to detect hazardous conditions. Computers can monitor for such hazards as fire, gas releases, and excess heat and pressure. Computerized data banks help safety personnel stay up-to-date on the laws, regulations, trends, research, and new information that affect their industries. Expert systems are computer tools that can help safety personnel form decisions, especially regarding topics in which they do not have

Copyright © Mometrix Media. You have been licensed one copy of this document for personal use only. Any other reproduction or redistribution is strictly prohibited. All rights reserved.

expertise. Computer-aided design and drafting can chart hazardous areas and safety systems on maps.

## Cold environment

A cold environment can be measured according to the air temperature, humidity, mean radiant temperature of surrounding surfaces, air speed, and core body temperature of people in extremely cold temperatures. The keys to preventing injury from cold environments are as follows:
- Modifying the environment by providing heat sources and using screens or enclosures to reduce wind speed.
- Adjusting activities to minimize time in cold areas and requiring regular breaks in a warm area.
- Providing protective clothing with insulated layers that both wick away moisture and provide a windscreen.
- Providing gloves, hats, wicking socks, and insulated boots to protect vulnerable extremities.
- Allowing employees time to become acclimated to the cold environment.
- Training employees on practices and procedures for staying safe in a cold environment.

## Hazard control

### Warnings, procedures, and personal protective equipment
Warnings, procedures, and personal protective equipment can all be part of a safety effort to reduce hazards. However, none of these choices should be the only means used to control a hazard because they all rely on human behavior. Warnings let people know when there is a dangerous situation and the people must then take appropriate action. Warnings can include alarms, flashing lights, sirens, labels, etc. For a warning to be effective, the following must be true:
- The warning must work.
- Someone must see the warning.
- The person who sees the warning must know what to do and then do it.

Procedures also require people to act. Good procedures can minimize danger if people use them. For procedures to be effective, the following is required of users:
- Know that a procedure is available for the hazardous situation.
- Find, understand, or remember the procedure.
- Follow the procedure correctly.

The effectiveness of personal protective equipment also depends on human behavior: people must choose correct equipment that fits well and they must use it and wear it correctly.

### Housecleaning, housekeeping, and sanitation
Housecleaning refers to the process of cleaning an area: sweeping, wiping surfaces, throwing away trash, etc. Housekeeping means putting things away where they belong. Every tool, piece of equipment, and material should have a designated storage area. Hazardous materials should have special storage areas designed specifically for them.

- 45 -

Copyright © Mometrix Media. You have been licensed one copy of this document for personal use only. Any other reproduction or redistribution is strictly prohibited. All rights reserved.

Sanitation means ensuring the facility is clean and germ-free. It includes such issues as the following:
- Safe drinking water.
- Clean working toilets.
- Clean areas to prepare and eat food.
- Insect and rodent control.

Housecleaning, housekeeping, and sanitation can all reduce hazards. For example, putting equipment where it belongs means that no one is going to trip over that item and the item cannot fall on anyone. Providing a sanitary environment also reduces disease transmission and can lessen exposure to hazardous substances.

**Protecting controls from being accidentally activated**

Controls that are activated accidentally can sometimes have serious or dangerous consequences. Several methods are available for preventing controls from being accidentally activated. Push-button or toggle controls should be recessed below the surface of a control panel so they can't accidentally be pushed or switched. Perimeter guards between or around push buttons can stop a worker from accidentally pressing two buttons at once. Guards over a control keep it from being pushed accidentally. These are common for foot controls that could be activated if something fell on the control. Isolating controls from other controls and from traffic areas can keep them from being bumped and accidentally activated. Controls can also be positioned on a control panel so that normal movement around them does not activate them. A control can be locked so that resistant force, a specific sequence of events, or a key control is needed to activate the control.

**Preventing damage from ionizing radiation**

The damage caused by ionizing radiation depends on the type and dose of the radiation, the tissue and organs exposed, and the age of person being exposed. The best way to control potential damage is to limit the amount of radiation people are exposed to by limiting the amount of source material. It is also important to limit the amount of time people are exposed to radiation. Other ways to reduce exposure to ionizing radiation include the following:
- Increasing the distance between people and sources of ionizing radiation.
- Using shielding such as air, hydrogen, and water to protect people from sources of radiation. The material used as a shield depends on the type of radiation.
- Using barriers such as walls and fences to keep people away from sources of radiation.
- Use liners and protective materials to keep contaminated waste from leaching into groundwater.

<u>Warnings, evacuation, security, dosimetry, training, and system design and analysis</u>
Warnings need to mark any areas where ionizing radiation is located as well as equipment that uses ionizing radiation. In addition to signs on these areas, flashing lights and audio signals can serve as additional warnings. Evacuation is a tool used to remove people from an area where a significant amount of ionizing radiation has been released. Security procedures need to be in place to keep sources of ionizing radiation from getting into the wrong hands. Procedures can include physical monitoring, controlled entry and exit, and

Copyright © Mometrix Media. You have been licensed one copy of this document for personal use only. Any other reproduction or redistribution is strictly prohibited. All rights reserved.

manifest systems. Dosimetry measures people's exposure to ionizing radiation. It is necessary because we cannot see or feel this radiation. People who work with or near ionizing radiation need training about its hazards and how to protect themselves and others. System design and analysis can help prevent dangerous exposure to ionizing radiation by anticipating and preventing possible sources of failure.

## Hazards during the maintenance and repair of items and hazards due to poor communication

Planning for safety during the normal use of a product is necessary, but is not enough. Safety must also be considered when a product is being repaired or maintained. Hazards during maintenance and repair can occur because of the following:

- A repair and maintenance schedule is either not available or not correct.
- Safety features such as accessible service points and manual power options are not included in the product's design.
- Poorly written or incorrect maintenance and repair procedures lead to the maintenance or repair being done incorrectly.

Poor communication can lead to hazards when instructions and warnings are not clearly and correctly communicated to co-workers, managers, supervisors, customers, and end-users of a product.

## Hazards related to color and signage

Color is used for marking hazards and relating information through color-coding. However, hazards related to color can occur because of color blindness. In addition, everyone must understand and remember what different colors stand for. However, American National Standards Institute (ANS), Department of Transportation (DOT), and Occupational Safety and Health Administration (OSHA) all have standards designating what different colors symbolize. Following these standards helps workers remember what colors mean. Signs can also mark hazards and provide safety information. To be effective, signs need to be multilingual and standardized. It is also helpful to include symbols along with text or as a replacement for text. OSHA, Consumer Product Safety Commission (CPSC), International Organization for Standardization (ISO), Association for the Advancement of Medical Instrumentation (AAMI), and other federal agencies provide standards for signage. Following standards for color and signage enables workers to quickly and easily understand the warning or hazard that is being communicated.

## Personal protective equipment

Personal protective equipment is any specialized clothing or equipment worn or used to protect a person from hazards. Personal protective equipment can include HAZMAT suits, goggles, gloves, respiration equipment, hard hats, and more. Personal protective equipment can form an essential part of a safety plan, but it should never be a primary means for controlling hazards. Personal protective equipment forms a barrier between the user and a hazard, but it does not remove the hazard. It is far better to remove the hazard, if possible. Personal protective equipment has limited success because the user must have the right equipment and know how to use it properly, often in an emergency situation. In addition, the personal protective equipment must fit properly and must be well-maintained.

Copyright © Mometrix Media. You have been licensed one copy of this document for personal use only. Any other reproduction or redistribution is strictly prohibited. All rights reserved.

## Successful personal protective equipment program

In order to be effective, a program for personal protective equipment must include detailed, written procedures that address how to select, manage, use, and maintain personal protective equipment. These procedures must be enforced and supported by management and should include standards and rules for the following:

- Wearing and using personal protective equipment.
- Inspecting and testing personal protective equipment to ensure it is in good condition and working properly.
- Maintaining, repairing, cleaning, and replacing personal protective equipment.

Another important element of a personal protective program is to ensure that users understand and accept the importance of personal protective equipment. Allowing users to participate in selecting the personal protective equipment they will wear can help them "buy into" the program and be more likely to use their personal protective equipment when it is needed.

## Equipment to protect eyes and hearing

Eyes need to be protected from flying particles and objects, splashing liquids, excessive light, and radiation. Types of eye protection include spectacles, with or without side shields, and goggles. Spectacles and goggles protect the eyes from frontal impact injuries, particles, splashes, etc.  Side shields are needed for spectacles if there is any danger of particles hitting the eyes from the side. Spectacle lenses can be tinted to prevent light damage and include radiation filters. Different types of spectacles and goggles are available for different tasks. For example, employees working with lasers need laser safety goggles that can filter the specific wavelength and intensity of the laser beam. Hearing needs to be protected from excessive noise, or hearing loss can result. Two main types of hearing protection are muffs and earplugs. Muffs are best for very noisy environments. For the noisiest environments, muffs and plugs can be used together.

## Equipment to protect the head and face

Personal protective equipment for the head can protect wearers from being hit by falling or flying objects, from bumping their heads, and from having their hair caught in a machine or set on fire. Helmets bump caps, and hard hats are examples of this type of head protection. Hoods and soft caps are another type of head protection that also protects the face and neck. Hoods may include hardhat sections as well as air supply lines, visors, and other protective features. They provide protection from heat, sparks, flames, chemicals, molten metals, dust, and chemicals. Head protection can also aid sanitation by keeping hair and skin particles from contaminating the work. This is especially important in processes involving food and clean room work. Hairnets and caps offer this type of protection. Face shields and welding helmets protect the face from sparks, molten metal, and liquid splashes. They should always be used in conjunction with eye protection such as goggles or spectacles.

## Protection for hands, fingers, arms, feet, and legs

Hands, feet, arms, fingers, and legs need protection from heat and cold, sharp objects, falling objects, chemicals, radiation, and electricity. Gloves and mittens protect the hands and fingers and can even extend up the wrist and arm. They can be made of different materials according to the protection needed: for example, lead is used for radiation protection and leather for protection from sparks. Gloves can be fingerless to protect just the hands; finger guards are used to protect just the fingers.  Creams and lotions also protect hands and

Copyright © Mometrix Media. You have been licensed one copy of this document for personal use only. Any other reproduction or redistribution is strictly prohibited. All rights reserved.

fingers from water, solvents, and irritants. Feet can be protected by the appropriate type of shoes: safety shoes with steel toes and insoles; metatarsal or instep guards; insulated shoes; and slip-resistant, conductive, or non-conductive soles. Rubber or plastic boots provide protection against water, mud, and chemicals while non-sparking and non-conductive shoes are useful for people working around electricity or where there is a danger of explosion. Shin guards and leggings protect legs from falling and moving objects and from cuts from saws and other equipment.

Equipment for the body
Personal protective equipment for the body provides protection from hazardous materials, biohazards, heat, fire, sparks, molten metal, and dangerous liquids. This clothing is often combined with other types of personal protective equipment, such as respiratory equipment and eye protection. Types of personal protective equipment for the body include the following:
- Coats and smocks to protect clothing from spills
- Coveralls, which may include hoods and boots
- Aprons, which protect the front of a person from spills and splatters
- Full body suits for working with substances that present a danger to life or health (may include cooling units to help lower the wearer's body temperature)
- Fire entry suits
- Rainwear
- High-visibility clothing for people working on road construction or in traffic
- Personal flotation devices for people working around or on water
- Puncture-resistant or cut-resistant clothing for protection from ballistic objects, power saws and other cutting equipment
- Some personal protective equipment is designed to be disposable, especially clothing contaminated with hazardous materials.

Respiratory protection
Respiratory protection can mean ensuring that air for breathing is of good quality or it can mean cleaning air before it is inhaled. Two types of equipment ensure that air is of good quality: self-contained respirators and supplied-air respirators. Air-purifying respirators clean air before it is inhaled. Self-contained breathing apparatuses (SCBA) are an example of a self-contained respirator. SCBAs are usually enclosed in a backpack and provide users with clean, breathable air. Hose masks, air-line respirators, and air-supplied suits and hoods are all examples of supplied-air respirators. These units provide breathable air to the wearer through a hose from an outside source. Air-purifying respirators use filters, cartridges, or canisters to remove particulates and gases from air. Different types of filters, cartridges and canisters are available for different types of contaminants.

Copyright © Mometrix Media. You have been licensed one copy of this document for personal use only. Any other reproduction or redistribution is strictly prohibited. All rights reserved.

# Recognizing Hazards

**Human factors theory of accident causation**

According to the human factors theory of accident causation, accidents are caused by human error resulting from the following:
- Overload.
- Inappropriate response.
- Inappropriate activities.

Overload occurs when a person's responsibilities are greater than their capacity at that moment. Note a person's capacity can change and depends on natural ability and training, state of mind, physical condition, and stress levels. The following factors can also affect capacity:
- Environmental factors such as noise and temperature.
- Situational factors such as clarity of the instructions and level of risk.

Inappropriate response refers to any actions before or after an accident that cause the accident or make it more severe. For example, seeing a hazard and not correcting it. Inappropriate activities include jobs for which a person is not trained.

**Causes of emergencies**

Natural emergencies stem from floods, earthquakes, dust storms, tornadoes, and other natural events. Fires and explosions are another type of emergency. Fires can be especially dangerous in populated areas or in areas with hazardous materials. In addition, fires can lead to explosions. Explosions are dangerous because they can damage a wide area. System failures can create emergencies because they can lead to fire, explosion, release of hazardous materials, and other dangerous situations. Traffic problems and transportation accidents can cause emergencies when they block traffic or spill hazardous materials. People's behavior is another cause of emergencies. Both intentional and unintentional actions can cause emergencies. For example, terrorists can deliberately cause emergencies. Unintentional actions could include pressing or rushing to enter or leave a crowded area. The final major cause of emergencies is military action.

**Causes of accidents**

The most common causes of accidents, according to Hartshorne, include the following:
- Personal beliefs and feelings – feeling invincible, ignoring rules and procedures, etc.
- Decision to work unsafely – a conscious decision to work unsafely.
- Mismatch or overload – worker is in poor physical condition or is stressed and tired, the work is too complex or too repetitive, the work environment is too hot or noisy, etc.
- Systems failure – management failure to provide clear policies and procedures, to correct hazards, to offer training, etc.
- Traps – poorly designed workstations, defective equipment, inadequate lighting and ventilation, etc.

Copyright © Mometrix Media. You have been licensed one copy of this document for personal use only. Any other reproduction or redistribution is strictly prohibited. All rights reserved.

- Unsafe conditions – whether caused by the injured person, a co-worker, management, the weather, etc.
- Unsafe acts – using drugs and alcohol on the job, using incorrect tools and equipment, forgetting correct procedures, etc.

## Burns

A burn occurs when heat is applied to body tissues faster than the body can dissipate it. When this happens, the body tissue stores the excess energy, causing the temperature of the tissue to rise and leading to discomfort or pain. The traditional way to classify burns is according to their appearance as first-, second-, or third-degree. A first-degree burn is superficial with some reddening and pain. Healing takes 5-10 days. A second-degree burn is deep with blisters and pain. Healing can take as long as a month. With a third-degree burn, the skin is destroyed and healing can take many months. There is actually less pain with a third-degree burn. A newer way to classify burns is according to the depth of the tissue that is damaged. According to this classification, burns are considered superficial, deep, or full.

## Principles of hazard control

The first two principles of hazard control are as follows:
- Recognize hazards.
- Select preventive actions.

Recognizing hazards usually requires a team approach, as no one person can know all the possible hazards. This step includes such tasks as knowing how materials interact, understanding the use environment, and anticipating user behavior patterns.

Selecting preventive actions can include
- Eliminating the hazard, whether by changing a process, design, material, etc.
- Reducing the severity of the hazard.
- Reducing the probability that the hazard will occur.
- Designing redundancy into the system through backup systems, parallel subsystems, etc.
- Installing safety devices such as machine guards and fail-safe devices.
- Installing warning devices.
- Developing safe procedures.
- Requiring personal protective equipment.

## Common environmental hazards

Common environmental hazards include
- Heat
- Light
- Noise/Vibration
- Pressure
- Chemicals
- Radiation

Copyright © Mometrix Media. You have been licensed one copy of this document for personal use only. Any other reproduction or redistribution is strictly prohibited. All rights reserved.

These hazards can be especially problematic because of the following:
- Effects are generally cumulative and only appear over time.
- Effects cannot be observed directly.
- Effects may be delayed and not be apparent until years later.

Effects may be physical, such as burns, illnesses, and hearing loss, or behavioral, such as irritability or nervousness. Controlling environmental hazards requires recognizing that a hazard exists, knowing the severity of the hazard, and knowing the length of time that a person can be safely exposed to the hazard at that level. Laboratory and field instruments are generally needed to determine whether a hazard exists and its severity. For example, instruments can measure the noise level of a piece of equipment and determine whether that equipment poses a danger to the workers' hearing abilities.

**Routes through which hazardous substances enter the body**

Hazardous substances enter the body through three routes: inhalation, ingestion, and absorption through the skin. Inhalation means breathing the hazardous substance into the upper respiratory system and lungs. From there, gases and vapors can enter the bloodstream and be transported throughout the body while solid particles are either expelled from the respiratory tract or become lodged in the alveoli. Ingestion means eating or drinking materials. Ingested materials travel to the intestinal tract and are then absorbed into the bloodstream. Absorption through the skin means that hazardous materials enter the bloodstream directly through cuts and abrasions or vulnerable skin areas. In addition to these three main sources of entry, the eyes and skin can also be directly harmed by contact with hazardous chemicals. Skin disorders can include cracking, sores, reddening, and acne. Eyes can be irritated and develop conjunctivitis or more serious injuries.

**Factors affecting transportation hazards**

Design and safety features for vehicles help increase safety. Such features are established and enforced by the National Highway Traffic Safety Administration (NHTSA), Federal Motor Vehicle Safety Standards (FMVSS), Society of Automotive Engineers (SAE), Department of Transportation (DOT), and Federal Highway Administration (FHA). These devices include antilock brakes, airbags, automatic seat belts, warning indicators, and automatic headlights. Operators (drivers) also affect safety when driving. People become better drivers by taking driver training courses, driver's education and defensive driving). On the other hand, driving drunk, under the influence of drugs, or even while talking on a cell phone can reduce the safety of drivers. Facilities include highway designs and traffic control devices as follows:
- Signage
- Traffic lights
- Lane markings
- Traffic separation devices and barriers
- Guardrails
- Protected bridge supports

Copyright © Mometrix Media. You have been licensed one copy of this document for personal use only. Any other reproduction or redistribution is strictly prohibited. All rights reserved.

The driving environment includes the following:
- Time of day is a factor in accidents. More accidents occur at night when visibility is lower. Weather conditions affect driving. Rain and snow hinder visibility and make the road slippery.
- Road conditions, such as potholes, can affect safety.
- Driving distractions such as eating, listening to music, talking to passengers, and talking on cell phones can cause unsafe driving.

## Hazards for railroads, aviation, and pipelines

Hazards from railroads stem from derailments (especially if toxic materials are released) and grade-crossing accidents with vehicles. Safety features in railroads include the following: Ladders with slip-resistant rungs, Grab bars, Slip-resistant walkways and handrails, Insulated tank cars to prevent heat build-up and explosions, Interlocking couplings and warning placards for cars carrying hazardous materials, Protected grade crossings. Aviation hazards include the following: Mechanical failures, Crowded airspace during takeoff and landings, Leaking fuel tanks, Weather conditions such as wind shear and ice. Safety features in aviation include the following: Technology such as on-board computers and instruments for navigation, fire detection, collision avoidance, pressurization, etc., Air traffic control systems, Flight staff and air traffic controller training and certification, Strict design and maintenance standards for aircraft. Hazards in pipelines include leaks, fires, and explosions. Controls include strict design, operation, inspection, maintenance, and reporting procedures and standards, according to the material being transported.

## Common causes of work injuries

The most common causes of work injuries are the following:
- Overexertion.
- Impact accidents (where the injured person is struck by an object).
- Falls from heights.
- Reaction to chemicals.
- Compression.
- Motor vehicle accidents.
- Exposure to caustics, radiation, or extreme temperatures.
- Abrasion or rubbing.
- Slips and trips.

Sprains and strains are the most common injury experienced at work followed by bruises, cuts, and fractures. The back is the most frequently injured part of the body, largely because of improper lifting techniques. The next most frequently injured parts of the body are the legs (including knees and ankles), fingers, and arms. Workplace injuries caused by repetitive motion have also increased as more jobs require computer use.

## Dose threshold, lethal dose, lethal concentration, irritants, narcotics, and anesthetics

Dose threshold is the minimum dose of a substance needed to produce a measurable effect. Thresholds are determined, in part, by observing changes in body tissues, growth rates, food intake, and organ weight. Lethal dose is the amount of a substance that is likely to

Copyright © Mometrix Media. You have been licensed one copy of this document for personal use only. Any other reproduction or redistribution is strictly prohibited. All rights reserved.

cause death. The lethal dose of a substance is determined by testing on animals. Lethal concentration is the amount of an inhaled substance that is likely to cause death. Irritants are substances that irritate the skin, eyes, and the inner linings of the nose, throat, mouth, and upper respiratory tract. These substances do not do any irreversible damage. Narcotics and anesthetics keep the central nervous system from operating correctly. Used at the right dose, these substances cause no serious or irreversible effects. However, if too much of the substance is used, unconsciousness or death can result.

**Biohazard, bacteria, virus, fungi, rickettsia, parasite, and bloodborne pathogens**

Biohazards are biological hazards that are toxic or allergenic and that come from plants or animals. Bacteria are one-celled organisms that are so small that they are invisible to the eye. Bacteria multiply by simple division and come in many shapes: cylindrical or rod-shaped, a string of beads, or spiral or corkscrew. Many bacteria, such as those that aid digestion, are useful. Viruses are small parasitic organisms that need a host cell in order to develop and reproduce. Viruses are usually transmitted through contact. Fungi are parasitic species that can grow on either dead or living hosts and range in size from microscopic to large. Rickettsia is rod-shaped microorganisms that are smaller than bacteria. They live in a host cell and depend on the host to develop and reproduce. Examples of parasites include tapeworms and liver flukes. Parasites live in or on other plants and animals. Bloodborne pathogens are micro-organisms that live in human blood and can cause diseases such as hepatitis B.

The primary danger from biohazards is infection. This occurs when biohazardous agents enter the body or skin. This can occur through ingestion, puncture wounds, skin contact, or inhalation. There is no treatment or cure for some biohazard infections, making training, procedures, and equipment designed to protect workers very important. Laboratories that use biohazards must keep them contained so workers and other people aren't exposed to any potentially hazardous materials. Workers must be trained on what hazards the materials they work with present and how they can protect themselves from these hazards. In addition, safety equipment such as enclosed containers, safety cabinets, and personal protective equipment must be available. Robots can also be used to perform many functions, reducing the contact people need to have with biohazards. Facilities can also be designed to reduce or eliminate hazards by including barriers and separate laboratories for working with biohazards.

**Gas leaks**

One common cause of gas leaks is dirt on valves, threads, gaskets, and other closures. The dirt contamination keeps the closures from closing properly. Another cause is overpressurization. If a gas vessel is too full, the closures can distort and separate from the gaskets. The vessel can then crack, leading to a gas leak. Excessive heat and cold can also cause gas leaks, especially if the gas vessel is composed of dissimilar metals that are joined. If the metal heats or cools at different rates, the joint can weaken and crack, allowing gas to escape. Operator error can also lead to gas escapes. This type of error occurs when the operator does not close the valves properly or opens them at the wrong time. Some techniques to detect gas leaks include scents added to the gas, cloth streamers, leak detectors, and thermometers. Sometimes operators detect a leak because they hear the gas escaping or they see corrosion on the gas vessel.

Copyright © Mometrix Media. You have been licensed one copy of this document for personal use only. Any other reproduction or redistribution is strictly prohibited. All rights reserved.

**Chemical hazards**

Chemicals are a part of life with over three million compounds registered. Some of these compounds are dangerous and some are not. Three factors to remember when thinking about chemical hazards are as follows:
- Compounds that are known hazards may not be dangerous at low concentrations.
- Compounds that normally aren't dangerous may become dangerous when used in certain ways.
- Compounds that aren't normally dangerous may become dangerous when mixed with other compounds.

Chemical regulations and standards have helped improve indoor air quality by banning smoking in public places and addressing mold and allergy issues and required ventilation. Regulations have also improved outdoor air and water quality by controlling hazardous materials and regulating clean-up actions. Other regulations and hazards address food, cosmetics, and other consumer products.

The following are terms related to chemical hazards:
- Latency period - Latency period is the amount of time between exposure to a chemical and observable effects from that chemical. The effects may be immediate, as with a chemical burn, or delayed, as with cancer.
- Acute exposure - Acute exposure refers to disease or effects that occur after only one exposure to a chemical.
- Chronic exposure - Chronic exposure refers to disease or effects that occur only after repeated exposure to a chemical.
- Local effects - Local effects are effects from a chemical that injure the skin, eyes, or respiratory system.
- Systemic effects - Systemic effects are effects from a chemical that damage organs or biological functions.
- Asphyxiants - Asphyxiants are materials that displace oxygen, interfering with breathing and oxygen transport in the blood.
- Nuisance dusts - Nuisance dusts cause irritation and coughing but have no long-term dangerous effects on the body.
- Carcinogens - Carcinogens are substances that produce cancer in animals or humans.
- Mutagens - Mutagens are substances that change the genetic structure of an animal or human, affecting the health of future generations.
- Teratogens - Teratogens are substances that cause a fetus to be malformed.

**Chemical burns**

Most chemical burn injuries occur in the manufacturing industry, service industry, trade, and construction. Chemical burns can be caused by numerous chemicals, including the following:
- Acids and alkalines.
- Soaps and detergents.
- Cleaning compounds.
- Solvents.
- Degreasers.

Copyright © Mometrix Media. You have been licensed one copy of this document for personal use only. Any other reproduction or redistribution is strictly prohibited. All rights reserved.

To prevent chemical burns, a safety program must:
- Educate workers and supervisors about the chemicals they are using.
- Require the correct personal protection equipment for the chemical being used.
- Educate workers and supervisors on how to correctly use and maintain the personal protection equipment.
- Monitor the use of personal protection equipment to ensure that it is being used properly.
- Monitor the use of personal protection equipment to ensure that it is replaced when it passes its useful life.

## Dust explosions

Dust explosions occur when fine particles of a material disperse in the air and then ignite. The dust can become airborne during a normal working procedure or when dust that has settled in a room is disturbed. Such explosions can occur in a series with an initial explosion disturbing settled dust, causing it to become airborne and ignite. In addition, oxidizing agents in the air can make a dust explosion even more severe.

Most organic dusts are combustible in the air, as are some inorganic and metallic dusts. The severity of the explosion depends on numerous factors:
- Type of dust.
- Size of the dust particles (Smaller particles ignite more easily).
- Concentration of particles in the air (Higher concentrations of particles are more flammable).
- Presence of oxygen (More oxygen pressure increases the likelihood of an explosion).
- Presence of impurities (Inert materials mixed in with the dust reduces its combustibility).
- Moisture content (Moisture increases the ignition temperature, making combustion less likely).
- Air turbulence (Combustion occurs more readily and explosions are more severe when air turbulence mixes the dust and air together).

## Ignition temperature, combustion point, exothermic chemical reactions, endothermic chemical reactions, heat transfer, spontaneous combustion, and hypergolic reactions

Ignition temperature and combustion point both refer to the point at which a fuel bursts into flame. Exothermic chemical reactions create more heat than they consume while endothermic chemical reactions consume more heat than they create. Heat transfer is the movement of heat from a higher temperature to a lower temperature. This can occur by conduction, radiation, or convection. Conduction is direct thermal energy transfer, radiation is electromagnetic wave transfer, and convection is heat transfer through the movement of hot gases. Spontaneous combustion occurs when the natural decomposition of materials lead to higher temperatures and fire. Hypergolic reactions occur when fuels are mixed. Oxidizers cause heat buildup and the fuels combust at room temperature.

## Resistance, conductors, insulators, current density, heating, and arcing

Resistance is the measure of a material's resistance to current flow. If there is more than one path for electricity to flow, it will always choose the path of least resistance. Conductors are materials that allow electricity to flow freely. Copper and water are both examples of

Copyright © Mometrix Media. You have been licensed one copy of this document for personal use only. Any other reproduction or redistribution is strictly prohibited. All rights reserved.

good conductors. Insulators are materials that do not allow electricity to flow easily. Rubber, glass, wood, air, and most plastics are insulators. Current density is the amount of current flowing through a particular cross section of a conductor. Heating is the tendency of conductors to heat up as electrical current flows through the material. Arcing is current flowing through the air between two conductors that aren't touching.

## Common electrical hazards

The most common electrical hazards are electric shock, heat and fire, and explosion. Electric shock occurs when a person becomes part of an electric circuit, allowing electricity to flow through the body. The severity of the shock depends on the type of current (alternating or direct), the amount of current, the length of exposure, and the part of the body through which the current passed. Heat and fire can occur when more current flows through a material than that material can handle. First, the material heats up. Then, the excessive heat can ignite flammable items in the area. Heat and fire can also occur because of poor connections and electrical shorts. Explosions occur when arcing takes place in an area with flammable vapors or combustible dust.

## Heat exhaustion, heat prostration, heat cramps, and heat fatigue

Heat exhaustion and heat prostration are different names for the same illness. They are caused by a victim failing to drink enough water to replace fluids lost to sweat when working in a hot environment. Symptoms include the following: cold, clammy skin; fatigue; nausea; headache; giddiness; and low, concentrated urine output. Treatment requires moving the victim to a cool area for rest and replacing fluids. Heat cramps are muscle cramps during or after work in a hot environment. They occur because of excess body salts lost during sweating. Treatment involves replacing body salts by drinking fluids such as sports drinks. Heat fatigue occurs in people who aren't used to working in a hot environment. Symptoms include reduced performance at tasks requiring vigilance or mental acuity. Victims need time to acclimate to the hot environment and training on ways to work safely in a hot environment.

## Heat illness, heat stroke, sunstroke, heat hyperpyrexia, heat syncope, and heat rash

A heat illness is any illness primarily caused by prolonged exposure to heat. Heat stroke occurs when a person's thermal regulatory system fails. Symptoms include lack of sweating, hot and dry skin, fever, and mental confusion. Victims need to be cooled immediately or loss of consciousness, convulsion, coma, or even death can result. Sunstroke is a type of heat stroke caused by too much sun exposure. Heat hyperpyrexia is a mild form of heat stroke with lesser symptoms. Heat syncope affects individuals who aren't used to a hot environment and who have been standing for a long time. The victim faints because blood flows more to the arms and legs and less to the brain. The victim needs to lie down in a cool area. Heat rash is also called prickly heat. It occurs when sweat glands become plugged, leading to inflammation and prickly blisters on the skin. Treatment can include cold compresses, cool showers, cooling lotion, steroid creams, and ointments containing hydrocortisone. During treatment, victims must keep their skin dry and avoid heat.

*Copyright © Mometrix Media. You have been licensed one copy of this document for personal use only. Any other reproduction or redistribution is strictly prohibited. All rights reserved.*

## Trenchfoot, chilblains, and hives

Trenchfoot occurs when a person spends an extended time as follows:
- Inactive.
- With moist skin.
- At temperatures that are cold but not freezing.

Bloods vessels in the feet and legs constrict, causing numbness, a pale appearance, swelling, and, eventually, pain. Treatment involves soaking the feet in warm water. However, the numbness can last for several weeks even after the feet are warmed. Chilblains are an itching and reddening of the skin caused by exposure to the cold. Fingers, toes, and ears are the most susceptible. Gentle warming and treatment with calamine lotion or witch hazel can lessen chilblains. Itchy red hives can occur in some people when their bodies develop an allergic reaction to the cold. The hives may be accompanied by vomiting, rapid heart rate, and swollen nasal passages. Cold compresses, cool showers, and antihistamines can help relieve the symptoms.

## Frostbite and hypothermia

Frostbite and hypothermia are the most dangerous cold hazards. Frostbite occurs when the temperature of body tissue goes below the freezing point. It leads to tissue damage. The amount of damage depends on how deeply the tissue is frozen. Severe frostbite can lead to the victim losing a damaged finger or toe. Frostbitten skin is usually white or gray and the victim may or may not feel pain. To treat frostbite, the damaged body part must be submerged in room-temperature water so it can warm up slowly. Hypothermia occurs when a victim's body temperature drops below normal. Symptoms include shivering, numbness, disorientation, amnesia, and poor judgment. Eventually, unconsciousness, muscular rigidity, heart failure, and even death can result. Warm liquids and moderate movement can help warm a victim who is still conscious. An unconscious victim needs to be wrapped warmly and taken for medical treatment.

## Soil

The following are properties of soil:
- Weight - Soil weight is the amount of solid material for a unit volume when the soil is dry. The soil needs to be dry because moisture content, which changes the weight of the soil, can change because of climate changes, compaction, and drainage.
- Density - Density is the weight of one cubic centimeter of soil.
- Internal resistance - Internal resistance depends on the friction and cohesion of the soil. It indicates the shear resistance of the soil.
- Internal friction - Internal friction also indicates the shear resistance of the soil. It must be less than internal resistance.
- Cohesion - Cohesion is the tendency of soil particles to cling together. Soil with high cohesion has higher internal tensile strength.
- Volume change - Volume change refers to the tendency of soils to shrink when they dry out and to expand when they get wet. When soil is compressed, the water is squeezed out and the soil dries, becoming smaller in volume.
- Consolidation - Consolidation is any process that reduces the water content of saturated soil.

Copyright © Mometrix Media. You have been licensed one copy of this document for personal use only. Any other reproduction or redistribution is strictly prohibited. All rights reserved.

The following are terms as they relate to soil:
- Bearing - Bearing refers to the load that soil can support. Along with footings, soil bears the weight of the building itself as well as its contents and extra forces caused by wind. Borings can help designers determine how big a load the soil in an area can bear.
- Piles - Piles are underground columns that transfer loads to the soil.
- Retaining walls - Retaining walls counteract the tendency of soils to exert lateral pressure.
- Angle of repose - Angle of repose is the natural angle that soil forms when it is piled up or when it collapses. This angle depends on the type of soil, the moisture content of the soil, and the presence of any other materials in the soil. Knowing the angle of repose is important for preventing cave-ins; creating walls with an angle less than the angle of repose is safer.
- Dewatering - Dewatering refers to any changes made to the moisture content of soil. Dewatering changes the volume of the soil and the amount of load the soil can bear.

### Infrared radiation, high-intensity visible light, and lasers

Sources of infrared radiation include fire, stoves, and heating elements. This radiation can cause eye disorders such as scotoma, swelling, hemorrhages, lesions, and cataracts. Controlling these dangers requires limiting exposure to the infrared radiation and wearing protective eye gear. Sources of high-intensity visible light include welding, carbon arc lamps, and some lasers. This type of light can damage the eyes. To prevent or control the damage, the following actions should be taken:
- Enclose the source of light.
- Limit the intensity of the source.
- Use shields, guards, or filters to protect eyes from the light source.
- Workers should wear protective eye gear.

Lasers are used in multiple fields, including construction, mining, health, and weapons. Lasers can damage the eyes and skin, depending on the laser's intensity, wavelength, and duration. To control the hazards related to lasers, the following actions should be taken:
- Enclose the laser source.
- Eliminate reflective surfaces.
- Require protective clothing and eye gear.
- Train users on safe procedures for using lasers.

### Microwaves and ultraviolet radiation

Microwaves are used in communications, drying, and navigation equipment as well as in microwave ovens. Microwaves pose a danger to eyes, causing cataracts to develop over time. Microwaves can also affect the central nervous system and interfere with cardiac pacemakers. To prevent microwave hazards, it is important to limit exposure whether by limiting the intensity of the microwaves or the length of exposure. You can also post warning signs and require protective clothing. Sources of ultraviolet (UV) radiation include the sun, heliarc welding, mercury and xenon discharge lamps, and full-spectrum fluorescent lamps. UV radiation can cause burns, skin reddening, and blisters. With extended exposure, skin cancer and skin aging can result and the cornea of the eye can become inflamed. Methods for controlling UV radiation hazards include the following:

Copyright © Mometrix Media. You have been licensed one copy of this document for personal use only. Any other reproduction or redistribution is strictly prohibited. All rights reserved.

- Limiting exposure to UV radiation, especially the most harmful wavelengths.
- Shielding skin and eyes from UV exposure through sunglasses, sunscreen, and protective clothing.

## Ionizing radiation

Ionizing radiation is radiation that can produce ions when it interacts with atoms and molecules. Types of ionizing radiation include x-rays, alpha particles, beta particles, gamma radiation, and neutrons. Ionizing radiation can come from natural sources, such as cosmic radiation and radioactive soils, and from artificial sources, such as television sets, diagnostic x-rays, and nuclear fuels. Exposure to ionizing radiation damages human cells, especially rapidly developing cells. It is especially dangerous for infants and children who have the most rapidly developing cells. Exposure to high doses of ionizing radiation causes radiation sickness characterized by weakness, sleepiness, stupor, tremors, convulsions, and, eventually, death. Low doses may cause more delayed effects, such as genetic effects, cancers, cataracts, and shortened life span.

## Overpressure devices

The following are overpressure devices used to control pressure in a pressurized container:
- Safety valves open when the upstream pressure is higher than a pre-set value. They are used for gas, steam, and vapor.
- Relief valves also open when the upstream pressure is higher than a pre-set value. They differ from safety valves in the following ways:
  - They are used for liquid.
  - The amount they open depends on the amount of overpressure.
  - They close automatically when the pressure returns to normal.
- Frangible discs are also called rupture discs. They are mounted between flanges in a vent pipe and burst at a particular pressure. They are used for liquids, gas, steam, and vapor.
- Fusible plugs are used in containers such as boilers and compressed gas cylinders. Because they are made of metal, they relieve pressure in a container when they melt.
- Discharge lines channel materials from a pressurized container or pressure relief device to a safe area.
- Vacuum failure devices keep vacuums from occurring in vent lines when a container is drained.
- Freeze plugs are used with water and water-based liquids. They work because these liquids expand when they come near their freezing point. As the liquid gets colder and expands, the freeze plug allows it to drain.
- Pressure changes as temperature changes; generally, pressure increases when temperature increases and decreases when temperature decreases. Temperature limit devices sense and control the temperature in a container in order to monitor and control the pressure.

## Low-pressure environments and high-pressure environments

A low-pressure environment is an environment with a lower pressure than occurs at sea level. Low-pressure environments occur at high altitudes and on aircraft. Hazards of low-

- 60 -

Copyright © Mometrix Media. You have been licensed one copy of this document for personal use only. Any other reproduction or redistribution is strictly prohibited. All rights reserved.

pressure environments include the following: sinus pain; loss of night vision; impaired memory, coordination, and judgment; drowsiness; euphoria; unconsciousness; and even death. To combat these hazards, the total pressure must be increased or the amount of oxygen in the breathing air must be increased. A high-pressure environment is an environment with a higher pressure than occurs at sea level. High-pressure occurs in underwater diving and some construction work such as tunneling. Hazards of high-pressure environments include nitrogen narcosis and decompression disorders such as dysbarism or the bends (bubble formation in tissues). To combat these dangers, breathing gases must be monitored for oxygen pressure, contaminant gases, and inert gases.

## High-pressure fluids

High-pressure fluids are used in such tools as paint sprayers, fire hoses, and fuel injection devices. Hazards associated with these fluids include air and gas injuries, injection injuries, and whipping of lines. Air and gas injuries occur when pressurized air or gases rupture or injure bodily tissues. Injection injuries occur when a stream of air, gas, or liquid penetrates the skin and enters the body. The fluid can be toxic, or injected gas can cause embolisms. Whipping occurs when fluid moving through a nozzle makes the muzzle and hose whip around. The hose and nozzle can hit people and property, causing injuries and damage. To reduce the hazards of high-pressure fluids, you can lower the pressure level, keep hydraulic lines away from people, use solid lines instead of hoses, and use shields or guarding to separate sprays from people and property. It is also important to train workers using high-pressure fluids in safety procedures they need to follow.

## Illumination

Illumination is the lighting of an area. Insufficient light can be a hazard leading to errors and accidents. However, overly bright lighting can injure the receptor cells in eyes. Moving from dark to bright areas of illumination (and vice versa) can also cause hazards because eyes need time to adjust to different light levels. Other illumination hazards include direct and reflected glare, flicker or strobe effects from flickering lights, and shadows. Individual vision abilities may cause difficulties. To help control these hazards, illumination levels need to be set according to the type of task and adjusted for the worker's age and vision. In addition, the type of lighting must be considered; guards can help shield workers' eyes from strobe effects and oscillating equipment. Workstations must be designed to eliminate glare, reflections, and the differences between the task and the surrounding environment.

## Structural failure

Structural failure occurs when a structure or part of a structure fails. The main types of structural failure include the following:
Shearing, Tension, Compression, Bending and buckling, Bearing, Impact, Material fatigue, Material change upon exposure to radiation, extreme temperatures, water, etc., Instability, Creep.


Structural failures can be caused by the following:
- Design errors, including incorrect computations, faulty material selection, etc.
- Non-homogenous materials, such as knots and grain in wood, voids in molded materials, and uneven distribution of materials in composite materials.

- 61 -

Copyright © Mometrix Media. You have been licensed one copy of this document for personal use only. Any other reproduction or redistribution is strictly prohibited. All rights reserved.

- Changes in material over time, such as changes in strength, brittleness, and ductility because of corrosion, rotting, wear, exposure to sunlight, etc.
- Physical damage through both use and abuse.
- Overloading.
- Poor assembly, maintenance, work habits, and other types of poor workmanship.

## Tripping hazards

Tripping is typically caused by a number of factors.
- Irregular surfaces such as warped floor boards uneven tile, and chipped concrete.
- Objects such as protruding nails sticking up from the floor.
- Objects such as tools and electrical cords left lying on the floor.
- Objects near the floor that intrude into a person's walking path, such as a low file drawer left open.

The following actions can be taken to reduce tripping hazards:
- Create and follow good housekeeping procedures such as putting tools away and promptly disposing of trash.
- Ensure that areas where the type of flooring changes are level.
- Avoid one- and two-step elevation changes.
- Post warnings in areas where the elevation changes.
- Repair damaged flooring.
- If electrical cords must temporarily cross walking paths, tape them down.

## Slipping hazards

A slip occurs when one or both feet slide on a surface. Slipping can occur because of the following:
- Polished shoes or floors.
- A change in floor conditions, going from dry to wet surfaces.
- A sloping surface.

To reduce slipping hazards, the following actions can be taken:
- Develop and follow good housekeeping procedures for promptly wiping up snow, ice, water, oil, oversprays, and any other materials that can make the floor surface slippery.
- Use drainage or elevated floors where wet processes are conducted.
- Use warning signs to indicate a change in surface conditions, such as when a floor is being mopped.
- Use mats and rugs to provide a transition area between wet and dry areas and to allow people to dry their shoes.
- Encourage employees to wear slip-resistant footwear.
- Choose slip-resistant floor materials.
- Use cleaning products that do not cause slipperiness.
- Install adhesive strips on stairs and slippery areas.

Copyright © Mometrix Media. You have been licensed one copy of this document for personal use only. Any other reproduction or redistribution is strictly prohibited. All rights reserved.

**Gangplanks and dock plates**

Gangplanks provide a path from a ship to a surface while dock plates provide a path from a vehicle to a surface. Both people and vehicles may travel across a gangplank or dock plate. Common hazards for both gangplanks and dock plates include the following:
- Slipping and tripping.
- Structural failure.
- Falls off the edge.
- Getting and staying in position.

To improve the safety of gangplanks and dock plates, the following actions should be taken:
- Label the load capacity of the gangplank/dock plate and ensure that capacity is not exceeded.
- Inspect the gangplank/dock plate regularly and repair or replace it if defects are found.
- Include a curb on the edge of the gangplank/dock plate so vehicles cannot run off the edge.
- Use anchoring methods such as stop pins or cleats to secure the gangplank/dock plate into position.

**Stairs and ramps**

Stairs are the most common way to move people from one elevation to another. To improve the safety of stairs, the following actions should be taken:
- Design enclosed stairs to reduce distractions as people walk down the stairs.
- In multi-story buildings, design staircases with landings so people can rest as they go up or down the flights of stairs.
- Keep the base of a stairway clean and free of hazards.
- Include handrails that will support a person's weight.

If the change in elevation is small, a ramp is preferable to stairs. When a staircase only has one or two steps, people often don't see it. To be safe, ramps must have the following features:
- Be made of a slip-resistant finish.
- Have a slope of less than 15 degrees (11 degrees for handicapped access).
- Include handrails or guardrails.
- Include landings if the ramp is long.

**Ladders and scaffolds**

Common hazards associated with ladders include the following:
- Falling off the ladder
- Slipping off the ladder rungs
- The ladder tipping over
- The ladder sliding
- Metal ladders conducting electricity.
To improve safety when using ladders, the following actions should be taken:
- Ensure that ladder rungs are slip-resistant

Copyright © Mometrix Media. You have been licensed one copy of this document for personal use only. Any other reproduction or redistribution is strictly prohibited. All rights reserved.

- Place ladders far enough from the wall so the arch of the foot can fit on the rung, not just the toe
- Inspect ladders frequently for damage such as cracks, bends, and other wear
- Anchor or tie ladders to a support structure
- Do not use metal ladders around electrical conductors.

Hazards associated with scaffolds include the following:
- Unsecured or loose planks
- Overloading and structural failure
- Tipping over
- Falls.

To improve safety when using scaffolds, the following actions should be taken:
- Select a scaffold that is rated for the load it will have to support
- Inspect scaffolds before use, checking planks, bolts, ropes, outrigger beams, bracing, and clamps
- Place the legs of the scaffold on a solid base.
- Tie the scaffold to a solid structure.

**Tools and machines**

Hazards associated with tools and machines include the following:
- Being struck by a tool, machine, or machine part.
- Being struck by flying debris from materials the tool or machine is acting on, such as concrete chips.
- Getting caught in a machine or tool.

Less direct hazards also exist. For example, if a machine requires repeated motion, cumulative stress disorders can result. For powered tools, electrical hazards are also present.

Tools and machines are a major source of injury, including the following:
- Cuts
- Abrasions
- Puncture wounds
- Tissue tears
- Crushing injuries
- Fractures
- Carpal tunnel syndrome
- Bursitis
- Tendonitis

As many as 8% of injuries involving lost time are related to hand tools.

<u>Machine motions that create machine hazards</u>
Machine motions that create machine hazards include:
- Rotating motion, such as the motion of the bit of a drill, can create a hazard. This type of motion can catch clothing, hair, and loose materials and wind it up. When a person's clothing or hair is caught, he or she can be pulled into the machine.

- 64 -

Copyright © Mometrix Media. You have been licensed one copy of this document for personal use only. Any other reproduction or redistribution is strictly prohibited. All rights reserved.

- Reciprocating (back and forth) and transverse (straight line) motion can create a hazard. People can become pinched or sheared between moving parts and nearby fixed objects.
- In-running nip points occur when machine parts rotate toward each other or when a machine part rotates toward a fixed component. Examples of these types of motions are found with belts and pulleys, gears, and conveyor belts, and rollers.
- Cutting actions, as with saws, lathes, and grinders can create a hazard.
- Punching, shearing, and bending motions, which occur when two machine components come together, can create a hazard.

<u>Machine guards</u>
Machine guards can serve multiple purposes:
- To keep people or their clothing from coming into contact with hazardous parts of a machine.
- To prevent flying debris from striking people.
- To muffle noise.
- To capture and enclose dust.
- To contain and exhaust contaminants.

To be effective, guards must be a permanent part of the equipment and must be durable enough to withstand the use environment. They must also not create additional hazards or interfere with the normal functions of the machine. Guards may include openings for inserting materials into a machine and for allowing access for inspections and maintenance. Such openings must be small enough so people cannot reach into hazardous parts of the machine.

## Hand tools

Use the following safe practices when using hand tools:
- Choose the appropriate tool for the job.
- Know the hazards of using the tool.
- Use tools correctly.
- Inspect, maintain, and repair or replace tools.
- Store tools properly.

Hand tool safeguards further protect users of hand tools. Safeguards include tool guards and handle designs. The length, shape, and material of a handle can all affect its safety:
- Long handles on axes and hatchets keep the tool away from the user so long swings can safely be used.
- Short handles on tools such as hammers allow for closer body work.
- Bent handles can help prevent repetitive motion and tissue compression disorders.
- High-friction plastic handles can help users grip a tool more tightly and can be molded to individual users.

## Robots

When workers enter a robot's work envelope (total area in which a robot's moving parts move), they can be struck by the robot, trapped between the robot and another surface, or hit by a tool or other object that the robot drops or ejects. To reduce these hazards, workers

Copyright © Mometrix Media. You have been licensed one copy of this document for personal use only. Any other reproduction or redistribution is strictly prohibited. All rights reserved.

should only enter a functioning robot's work envelope when they need to teach the robot a new motion. To keep workers safe when they do need to enter the work envelope, it needs to be well-lit with a clean floor that is clear of any obstructions. The work envelope needs to be kept clear of non-essential objects and any electrical and pneumatic components on the robot need to be covered by fixed covers and guards. Before entering the area, all lockout and test procedures need to be in place. Workers also need to ensure that they remove all tools and equipment from the work envelope when they leave.

## Powered vehicles

Powered vehicles for materials handling include forklifts, backhoes, bulldozers, etc. Hazards associated with these vehicles include the following:
- Visibility problems because operators cannot always see how well the load is positioned or whether other people or equipment are in the area.
- Falling loads, Overloading.
- Heating and fire from hot engines and exhaust.
- Tipping.

To reduce the dangers from powered equipment:
- Choose vehicles with a rollover protection system (ROPS) such as a rollover bar, cab, or seatbelts.
- Choose vehicles with a falling object protection system (FOPS) to protect operators from falling objects.
- Inspect, maintain, and repair powered equipment regularly.
- Train operators on how to safely use their equipment.
- Ensure good ventilation in areas where exhaust fumes could create a hazard.
- Ensure that pathways are clear of obstructions.
- Use mirrors to improve the operator's visibility.
- Someone should signal operator when visibility is limited.

## Jacks and hand-operated materials handling vehicles

Hazards associated with jacks include the following:
- Trying to lift a heavier load than the jack is designed to handle.
- Placing the jack on an unstable or soft surface.
- The jack slipping.
- The load shifting while on the jack.

To reduce the hazards associated with jacks:
- Use a strong enough jack for the load to be lifted.
- Place the jack on solid, hard surface where it cannot slip or sink.
- Stabilize, block, or anchor load being lifted so it will not shift.

Hazards for hand-operated vehicles include the following:
- Loads shifting, tipping, or falling
- Lack of visibility if the load is piled too high
- Hitting walls or other people with the hand-operated vehicle

Copyright © Mometrix Media. You have been licensed one copy of this document for personal use only. Any other reproduction or redistribution is strictly prohibited. All rights reserved.

To reduce the hazards, the following actions should be taken:
- Loads must be stable and secured.
- Loads must be low enough that the operator of the vehicle can see over them.
- Handles should include recessed areas, knuckle guards, or rubber bumpers to protect the operator's hands if the handles strike a wall.
- Operators' must allow safe maneuvering and stopping.

**Making a safe lift with a mobile crane**

In order to make a safe lift with a mobile crane, the operator needs to know the following:
- Whether the vehicle is level.
- Whether the outriggers are extended or retracted.
- If the outriggers are extended, whether they are supported by stable ground.
- Whether the tires are fully inflated.
- The angle of the boom.
- The length of the boom and jibs.
- The positions the boom will be in during the lift.
- The weight of the load.

With this information in hand, the operator can use a load chart to determine if the load is within the structural and stability limits of the crane.

**Hoisting apparatus, ropes, chains, and slings**

Hoisting apparatus can range from hand-operated derricks and winches to overhead cranes and aerial baskets. Hazards associated with hoisting apparatus include the following:
- Structural failure or tipping if the apparatus is overloaded or used on windy days
- Material falling on people or property below
- Limited visibility
- Use environment such as power lines.

To reduce the hazards associated with hoisting equipment, the following actions should be taken:
- Develop setup standards such as ensuring the setup site is level and away from power lines and that the apparatus is assembled properly.
- Ensure the apparatus is not overloaded. Train operators on both everyday and emergency procedures for using their equipment.

Ropes, chains, and slings are the rigging between the hoist and the load. Hazards associated with this rigging stem from the following:
- Overloading
- Deterioration
- Improper rigging leading to falls

To reduce these hazards, the following actions should be taken:
- Store rigging properly, out of sunlight and away from moisture and chemicals that can cause it to deteriorate.
- Inspect rigging regularly to ensure it is not deteriorating or wearing out.
- Follow load capacity charts for rigging to guard against overloading.

Copyright © Mometrix Media. You have been licensed one copy of this document for personal use only. Any other reproduction or redistribution is strictly prohibited. All rights reserved.

## Conveyors and bulk materials

Conveyors can be powered or manual. Hazards associated with conveyors include the following:
- Items falling off overhead conveyors onto people or items below.
- People being caught or pinched in moving parts.

To reduce these hazards, the following should be used:
- Overhead protection or enclosures to catch items that fall off the conveyor belt.
- Machine guards around pinch points.
- Emergency shutoff controls, interlock switches, and speed controls.
- Warnings at danger points along the conveyor belt.
- Appropriate tools for unjamming materials from chutes.
- Guardrails on any elevated walkways adjacent to overhead conveyors.

Bulk materials include such items as sand, soil, or grains. Hazards when working with these materials include cave-ins and a lack of breathable air. To control these hazards, the following actions should be taken:
- Restrain bulk materials by shoring or slanting the material at less than the angle of repose.
- Provide guardrails and a lifeline so people cannot fall into the bulk material.

## Elevators, escalators, and manlifts

Elevators, escalators, and manlifts are used to move people and goods up vertically. Hazards for elevators include the following:
- Becoming caught in the door.
- Falling down the elevator shaft.
- Being trapped in a stalled elevator.
- An elevator falling uncontrollably.
- Tripping when entering or exiting the elevator.

Elevators include numerous safety features to control these hazards, including brakes, interlocks, and emergency alarms. Elevators must be inspected regularly by trained elevator inspectors to ensure the elevators meet safety standards. The main hazard involving escalators is catching clothing or a body part between the steps and the side wall or between the steps and the floor at the top or bottom of the escalator. Escalators include emergency cutoff switches at the top and bottom to help control these hazards. They also have microswitches along the sidewall to cut power if something becomes caught between the steps and the wall. Hazards for manlifts include falling off the platform or becoming caught as the manlift moves through an opening in the floor. Operators must be trained on safe manlift procedures.

## Explosives

An explosive is a chemical compound or mixture used to create a rapid reaction that releases energy through heat and pressure. The Department of Transportation divides explosives into three categories:

Copyright © Mometrix Media. You have been licensed one copy of this document for personal use only. Any other reproduction or redistribution is strictly prohibited. All rights reserved.

- Class A explosives are the most dangerous type. These are explosives that possess a detonating hazard. Examples include black powder, dynamite, nitroglycerine, and some types of ammunition.
- Class B explosives are less dangerous because they function by rapid combustion instead of by detonation. Examples include fireworks, signal devices, smokeless powders, and some types of ammunition.
- Class C explosives are the least dangerous. Examples include certain types of fireworks and manufactured items that contain restricted amounts of Class A and/or Class B explosives.

The three main causes of damage and injury from explosions are blast wave effects, thermal effects, and fragment damage. Blast waves can hit objects and then reflect off and hit more objects with even more pressure. The severity of the damage from a blast depends on the pressure, duration, and drag force of the blast. Thermal effects stem from fireballs. Most fireballs reach a temperature of about 2,400 degrees Fahrenheit. Fragment damage is caused by pieces of material involved in the explosion scattering rapidly through the air. The amount of the scatter depends on the material involved: glass breaks and scatters easily while tougher materials don't scatter as much but may fly farther.

**Heat burns**

Heat burns occur most commonly in the manufacturing industry, especially in tasks involving welding and torch cutting. Major causes include the following:
- Flame
- Molten metal
- Asphalt and tar
- Steam and water

To reduce the risk of heat burns, a safety program must do the following:
- Include and enforce safety policies and procedures when working with heat hazards.
- Educate workers about heat hazards and about the safety policies and procedures.
- Provide correct personal protection equipment that is in good shape and train workers how to use the equipment properly.
- Ensure that employees have adequate workspace.
- Educate employees on how to use and maintain their tools.

**Flash point, lower flammable limit, upper flammable limit, and vapor volume**

Flash point is the lowest temperature at which a flammable liquid can form an ignitable mixture in air. If the source of ignition is removed, the vapor may stop burning. The lower flammable limit is the lowest concentration of vapor to air at which a flame will develop. At lower levels, the mixture is too lean to ignite. This is also known as the lower explosive limit. The upper flammable limit is the highest concentration of vapor to air at which a flame will develop. At higher levels, the mixture is too rich to ignite. This is also known as the upper explosive limit. Vapor volume refers to the amount of flammable vapor in the air above a flammable liquid. Generally, the liquid itself does not burn but the vapor above it burns.

Copyright © Mometrix Media. You have been licensed one copy of this document for personal use only. Any other reproduction or redistribution is strictly prohibited. All rights reserved.

## Powerlessness, mindlessness, normlessness, and meaninglessness

Powerlessness, mindlessness, and normlessness are all linked to automation in the workplace. Powerlessness is when workers feel like they can't control the work environment. Mindlessness occurs when workers do not have to think in order to perform their work. Normlessness is when workers feel disconnected from society's rules, norms, and mores. Meaninglessness is when workers feel a disconnection between their work and the finished product or service. These problems can lead to lower productivity and work quality. They are also linked to an increase in work-related accidents, absenteeism, turnover, and employee theft.

## Workplace stress

Stress is defined as the body's response to perceived threats. Stress can result in emotional problems such as anxiety and aggression, behavioral problems such as clumsiness and trembling, or cognitive problems such as problems concentrating or making decisions. Workplace stress is a serious problem, costing over $150 billion dollars a year. In fact, more than 15 percent of workplace disease claims are stress-related. In addition to contributing to accidents and injuries, stress is also linked to lower productivity, excess absenteeism and turnover, and poor morale. Workplace stress generally stems from s poor fit between the employee and the job. Specific issues can be poor physical working conditions, too much work or tasks that are too complex, lack of feedback or control over job responsibilities, unpredictable work schedules, and tense work relationships. In addition, personal and family problems can also contribute to workplace stress.

## Noise

The primary hazard of noise is hearing loss. Noise-induced hearing loss is related to the amount of time a person is exposed to the noise, the decibel level, the frequency, and whether the noise is continuous or intermittent. Types of noise-induced hearing loss include the following:
- Temporary threshold shift, which is caused by a short exposure to loud noise.
- Permanent threshold shift, which is caused by continuous exposure to noise.
- Temporary or permanent acoustic trauma caused by a loud noise, as from an explosion.

In addition to hearing loss, noise can also interfere with communication. Noise can make it difficult to hear warnings and sirens and even to communicate normally. It also interferes with learning, causes a startle response and other physiological problems such as high blood pressure and ulcers, and makes people irritable and frustrated.

### Baseline audiogram, decibel, hazardous noise, noise dose, noise-induced hearing loss, threshold of hearing, and threshold of pain

A baseline audiogram is a valid audiogram done after a quiet period and used as a comparison for future audiograms to see if hearing thresholds have changed. Decibel (dB) is a unit that defines the intensity of sound. Hazardous noise is any sound that can cause permanent hearing loss in a specified population. OSHA has established allowable daily amounts of noise that workers can safely be exposed to. The noise dose is the percentage of this daily exposure that a particular sound meets. A noise-induced hearing loss is any sensorineural hearing loss that can be linked to noise and for which no other cause can be

Copyright © Mometrix Media. You have been licensed one copy of this document for personal use only. Any other reproduction or redistribution is strictly prohibited. All rights reserved.

identified. Threshold of hearing is one dBA. This is the weakest sound that a healthy human can hear in a quiet setting. Threshold of pain is 140 dBA. This is the maximum level of sound that a human can hear without pain.

**Materials handling**

Materials handling involves lifting, moving, and placing items, whether manually or with equipment. Equipment frequently used for materials handling includes jacks, hoists, backhoes, escalators, derricks, and cranes. As many as 20-25 percent of disabling work-related injuries involve materials handling. Hazards stemming from materials handling differ depending on the material being handled and on the equipment used. Materials may be heavy, toxic, radioactive, hazardous, or flammable: each involves a different set of hazards. Equipment used may be mobile, such as a forklift, and could hit someone. Other times, items can fall off a hoist or a crane can collapse. Electrically powered equipment poses electricity hazards such as shock. Moving items manually also poses hazards. For example, lifting too heavy a load or using improper lifting techniques can cause sprains or strains.

Developing and enforcing procedures for materials handling can help reduce accidents. Procedures should include how to do the following:
- Select the correct equipment for the job.
- Communicate during the materials transfer, whether using hand signals, two-way radios, or other forms of communication.
- Deal with problems that could occur during the materials handling activity.

The procedures should also include step-by-step instructions for actually completing the materials handling activity.
Other actions that can help prevent materials handling accidents include the following:
- Create a safe materials handling environment with good lighting, wide aisles, and proper ventilation.
- Institute traffic controls to keep lift areas clear of people.
- Regularly maintain, inspect, and repair equipment used for materials handling.
- Train workers to properly use materials handling equipment, hand signals, and rigging.
- Train workers on safe techniques for manually moving materials, such as techniques for lifting heavy loads.
- Eliminate materials handling whenever possible.

<u>Safe lifting techniques</u>
Training workers on safe lifting techniques is important because improper lifting can cause sprain and strain injuries. As many as 25% of workers' compensation claims are for lower back injuries. To decrease the chances of injury when lifting, you need to do the following:
- Check the weight of the item to be lifted. If it is higher than the RWL (recommended weight limit), take steps to lighten the load, whether by using equipment to pick up the item or by splitting the load into two or more loads.
- Ensure the floor is not slippery.
- Spread your feet for a more stable stance.
- Keep your back straight.
- Hold the load close to your body.

Copyright © Mometrix Media. You have been licensed one copy of this document for personal use only. Any other reproduction or redistribution is strictly prohibited. All rights reserved.

- If an item is on the floor, bend down, grasp it firmly, and then stand up slowly and steadily.

RWL and LI
RWL stands for recommended weight limit. The RWL is the weight that healthy workers could lift for up to eight hours without causing musculoskeletal injuries. To calculate the RWL, you need to multiply LC (load constant) x HM (horizontal multiplier) x VM (vertical multiplier) x DM (distance multiplier) x AM (asymmetric multiplier) x FM (frequency multiplier) x CM (coupling multiplier). LI stands for lifting index. It measures the physical stress associated with lifting. As the LI goes up, the chance of injury also goes up. To calculate LI, you divide the load weight by the RWL. It is important to know the RWL and the LI because they can help you in the following ways:
- Identify tasks where injuries are more likely to occur.
- Help you develop procedures for safe lifting tasks.
- Identify which lifting tasks need to be redesigned first (generally those with higher LIs).

Ultimately, knowing the RWL and LI can lead to safer lifting procedures and fewer injuries. In order to determine the RWL, you must know the weight of the object. You must also know the following task variables:
- H (horizontal distance) – distance of the hands away from the midpoint between the ankles.
- V (vertical location) – distance of the hands above the floor.
- D (vertical travel distance) – number of inches or centimeters the object is lifted.
- A (asymmetry angle) – distance from 0 to 135 degrees that a worker turns during the lift.
- F (lifting frequency) – the average number of lifts per minute, measured over a 15-minute time span.
- C (coupling classification) – defined as good, fair, or poor depending on the type of grip (such as handles) and the type of container (box or bag; rigid or non-rigid, standard or irregular shape, etc.).

**Asbestos**

The first decision to make regarding asbestos in the workplace is whether it should be left alone or abated. If the asbestos is not friable and is not in an area where it will be disturbed, it may be safer to leave it alone. However, if the asbestos is friable or is, for example, in an area scheduled for renovation, then the asbestos-containing material (ACM) must be removed, enclosed, or encapsulated. If the decision is to leave the asbestos alone, an asbestos-monitoring program must be put in place to track whether the condition of the asbestos changes. Any work done with asbestos needs to be performed by trained and licensed personnel wearing high efficiency respirators and disposable personal protective equipment that covers the entire body.

Removing ACM is the most expensive choice, but once the ACM is removed, no further work or monitoring is needed. When ACM is removed, the area where it is located must first be enclosed in tough plastic walls. That area then must be ventilated by HEPA filtered negative air machines. The ACM is covered by a liquid solution that keeps asbestos fibers in place and is then put in leak proof containers for disposal. If ACM can be encapsulated, it is sprayed

- 72 -

*Copyright © Mometrix Media. You have been licensed one copy of this document for personal use only. Any other reproduction or redistribution is strictly prohibited. All rights reserved.*

with a sealant that binds the asbestos fibers together. The sealant hardens into a tough skin. ACM can also be enclosed. This involves placing airtight walls around the ACM. Warning signs need to be placed on the walls and their location needs to be marked on the building plans. If ACM is enclosed or encapsulated, an asbestos-monitoring program needs to be set up to track whether the condition of the asbestos changes.

## Problems linked to VDTs

Video display terminal (VDT) use is linked to eye fatigue, blurred vision, eyestrain, and nervousness. These eye problems can impair work performance, cause accidents, and lead to stress. In addition to eye problems, VDT use can also lead to cumulative trauma disorders. Setting up an ergonomic workstation helps to reduce VDT hazards. The keyboard should be located in front of the user and tilted so the back is lower than the front. The mouse should be placed within easy reach and the desk itself needs to be at a height so the user doesn't have to slouch. Changing work habits also helps. Employees need to be encouraged to take regular breaks and to use a soft touch on the keyboard and mouse. They should also avoid resting their wrists on any type of edge. Other helpful strategies include reducing lighting levels and minimizing glare.

## Repetitive strain and soft tissue injuries

Repetitive strain injuries, such as carpal tunnel syndrome, result from long-term, cumulative trauma to tendons, muscles, ligaments, joints, nerves, and other soft tissues. The hands, arms, neck, and shoulders are most subject to repetitive strain injuries. Other types of repetitive strain injuries include tendonitis, Raynaud's disease, and fibromyalgia. A safety program to reduce such types of injuries would include the following:
- Work processes and designs that are simple to understand and use, not overly demanding physically, and not boring or repetitive.
- Procedures designed to improve safety and reduce injuries.
- Training about the established procedures.
- Monitoring and analysis of procedures and injuries to evaluate any changes needed to the safety procedures.
- Workstation designs that can be adjusted to individual needs.
- Availability of correct tools for each worker and each task.

Copyright © Mometrix Media. You have been licensed one copy of this document for personal use only. Any other reproduction or redistribution is strictly prohibited. All rights reserved.

# Training and Management

**Promotion of safety by safety managers**

One way safety managers can promote safety is by actively involving employees in developing safety programs. Employees usually know what hazards exist. In addition, employees will participate more actively and enthusiastically in a program they help develop. A safety committee is a formal way that employees and managers can work together to develop and implement a safety program. Employees can also participate through suggestion programs. For a suggestion program to be successful, all suggestions must receive an answer; good ideas must be implemented, and the resulting cost and savings must be reported. Safety managers also promote safety by offering safety training to both new and current employees, posting safety signs, providing a good example, offering incentives, developing wellness programs, and promoting teamwork.

**Management's role in supporting safety**

Management support is crucial in order for a safety program to succeed. Both top management and middle management have a role in promoting safety in the workplace. Top management needs to issue safety policies and procedures so that all employees know how to be safe and know that management expects them to practice safe behavior. To facilitate safety, management needs to develop a reward system to reward employees who meet safety requirements and a reporting system for reporting anyone who isn't following safe procedures. Middle managers have a more hands-on role than top managers. They are responsible for directly reviewing employee safety performance, investigating accidents, setting an example of safe behavior, participating in safety meetings, and checking that employees are meeting safety goals.

**Need for training**

Accidents occur most frequently when employees are new to a job. New employees need to learn how to perform their jobs correctly and what procedures they should follow in case of an emergency. They also need to learn that safety is a priority in their company. Experienced employees need to receive training both to learn procedures that have changed and to reinforce procedures they have already learned. Supervisors and managers need to understand the hazards their workers face and the controls in place to protect the workers from harm. They must also be aware of laws and standards regulating their industry. Contractors need to know and understand the safety procedures of the company they are working with, as do the employees. Product users need to know how to safely use products they purchase. Manufacturers must provide clear instructions and safety warnings.

The main reason to provide training is that employees who receive training are less likely to make errors and have accidents. In addition, the Occupational Safety and Health Act (OSH Act) requires that employers provide safety and health training. Specific OSH Act training requirements include ensuring that employees know the following:
- How to use personal protective equipment.
- How to safely perform their duties in confined spaces.
- How to use respirators.

Copyright © Mometrix Media. You have been licensed one copy of this document for personal use only. Any other reproduction or redistribution is strictly prohibited. All rights reserved.

- How to use energy controls such as lockouts and tagouts.
- How to protect themselves from chemical hazards.

Training is often provided by either supervisors or safety and health professionals. Supervisors typically have the background to provide job-specific training while safety and health professionals can provide more general information. Other options for training include programmed instruction, interactive video and CD, and online training.

## Training objectives

Training is needed when a problem is due to lack of knowledge or skill but will not help when problems are due to poor procedures. Defining the objectives of training should be the first step in planning any training. An objective is defined as a statement that describes a needed change in the trainee. The objectives should be based on the desired outcome of the training and should clearly define the following:
- What actions the trainee needs to be able to accomplish as a result of the training.
- When, how, and where the trainee needs to be able to accomplish these actions.
- What criteria will be used to determine if the actions were performed to an acceptable level.

## Evaluating safety and health training

Whenever employees receive training, safety and health professionals need to know whether the training satisfied the training objectives. Therefore, the first step in evaluating the training needs to occur even before the training takes place. This involves setting a clear purpose and objectives for the training. Trainers should develop goals and write lesson plans that support those goals. Following the lesson plans should help ensure that the training meets its objectives. Evaluation can also be built into the training itself. Trainees can be tested to see what they have learned. Job performance and safety records can provide another way of evaluating training. Improving safety in the overall work environment is always an underlying goal of safety and health training. So training should result in fewer accidents and injuries, less time lost, and fewer health-related complaints.

## Adult learning vs. child learning

Occupational health and safety training is presented to adults, who learn quite differently from the way that children learn. Therefore, to craft more useful training courses, it is important to consider how adult learning differs from that of children. Adults learn from and apply their experience, whereas children have limited experience and are more receptive to the authority of the teacher. Adults are more self-directed in their learning, as they often see the benefits of learning and can pursue their interests. Children learn through play and are more likely to follow their play interests than to actively seek out information that they can apply in a novel way. Finally, adults are more goal-oriented in their learning than children are. Children are starting from a smaller base of knowledge and absorb whatever material is presented to them at an age-appropriate level. An understanding of these differences between adult learners and children can be used to craft more relevant training courses.

Copyright © Mometrix Media. You have been licensed one copy of this document for personal use only. Any other reproduction or redistribution is strictly prohibited. All rights reserved.

## Effective techniques for teaching adults

Well-designed training courses for adults will have at least three qualities: the training will be relevant to the group, it will provide current information not already known to the participants, and it will build upon their experience. Techniques that have proven useful to promote these three qualities include using hands-on experiences or exercises as a group or in small subgroups (for example, assembling a respirator), providing opportunities for discussion that honors the participants' experience, and allowing participants to demonstrate their newly acquired knowledge in a safe and nonjudgmental environment (for example, running a mock emergency scenario after the participants learn the principles of emergency response).

## Determining whether training course would be effective way

In determining whether a training course is an effective means of solving a specific problem faced by an organization, the organization should conduct a needs assessment. The first question to be answered is, What is the problem we are trying to solve? Once the problem is accurately identified, the organization can decide how best to solve it. Responses other than training courses that should be considered are:
- Designing visual aids to prompt workers to remember certain tasks; for example, one could post pictorial job procedures if employees continually forget the order of complex operations.
- Engineering solutions, such as providing different tools or equipment to do the task more safely. An example of this is to employ carts to move material rather than train people on proper lifting techniques.
- Redesigning the work sequence or procedure to eliminate hazards.

## Well-designed training course

A well-designed training course first must meet a demonstrated need for the organization to accomplish its objectives. For example, it must meet a regulatory requirement or convey information the organization has determined necessary to meet its production or financial goals. The course presentation should begin with a statement of the learning objectives so the course participants can obtain an overview of the course and the expectations. Secondly, the course leader should outline the regulatory or business objective the course will meet. The well-designed training course should use a variety of teaching methods to convey the information, such as PowerPoint presentations, small group activities, interactive discussions, and experiential learning. Using a combination of techniques keeps participants engaged and allows participants with different learning styles to benefit from the course material. Finally, all well-designed training courses have an assessment module to determine whether the participants have assimilated the information presented.

## Evaluating effectiveness of a training course

There are several effective methods to evaluate the effectiveness of a training course. The most well-known and traditional method is to administer a written quiz or exam at the end of the course that covers the information presented in the course. Some types of learning are best evaluated by requiring the course participant to demonstrate a newly acquired skill to the course instructor, such as how to perform CPR or how to wear an SCBA respirator. Requiring a team of coworkers to apply newly acquired knowledge in a tabletop exercise is

Copyright © Mometrix Media. You have been licensed one copy of this document for personal use only. Any other reproduction or redistribution is strictly prohibited. All rights reserved.

also an effective method of evaluating the effectiveness of a training course. An example of this type of evaluation is to require a group that has just received disaster planning training to plan for a specific disaster scenario as assigned by the instructor. What is important to remember when planning training evaluation tools is that methods other than written quizzes can be equally as effective and more useful to the participants.

## Well-designed presentation

A well-designed training presentation will first present an overview of the course content and will present the learning objectives of the course. The reason for the course will be stated, and participants will have an idea of how they will benefit from the course content. The course should be organized in a logical fashion, building knowledge as the course progresses. The instructor should build in short breaks at least every hour to give participants a chance to stand up and move around—this helps to combat boredom and refocus attention. The visual aids or PowerPoint presentation should also use a variety of slide types and varied content to keep the attention of the participants. For example, photographs and other visual aids should be incorporated into the presentation rather than using exclusively text. When text is used, it should be in a large font so that it is legible from a distance. Summary information and brief, informal quizzes should be presented frequently to provide feedback and opportunities to gauge whether the participants are assimilating the material.

## Effective presentation tools

Effective presentations use a variety of tools to achieve the best learning outcomes. Presenters will usually use a PowerPoint presentation or slides to convey the bulk of the information. When preparing PowerPoint presentations, it's important to ensure that the slides are not too wordy, and use a variety of graphics and pictures to add interest for the participants. In addition to PowerPoint presentations, demonstrations and hands-on tools are also important to effectively convey the information in an engaging way that enables learning. For example, have participants practice taking apart and putting together their respirator, or practice putting earplugs in correctly rather than illustrating it for them.

## ANSI/ASSE Z490.1

ANSI/ASSE Z490.1, American National Standard Criteria for Accepted Practices in Safety, Health and Environmental Training, is a professional standard for how to plan and conduct training programs in environmental health and safety. It is important in that it establishes best management practices for how training should be formulated, presented, and assessed. It sets an expectation that one will first determine whether the presentation of a training class is the best way to address the problem or situation facing the company. It then presents ways to evaluate the effectiveness of training and whether the training has furthered the objectives of the company in measurable ways. For example, has it increased compliance behaviors, decreased frequency of accidents, decreased worker's compensation costs, decreased turnover and absenteeism, or increased morale? In conclusion, the ANSI/ASSE Z490.1 standard sets the professional benchmark for conducting safety, health, and environmental training programs.

ANSI/ASSE Z490.1, American National Standard Criteria for Accepted Practices in Safety, Health and Environmental Training covers the following topics:

Copyright © Mometrix Media. You have been licensed one copy of this document for personal use only. Any other reproduction or redistribution is strictly prohibited. All rights reserved.

- Development of training courses: What are the reasons for training? What are the resources to be consulted in their development?
- Delivery of training courses: Elements of good presentations, considerations when delivering training to adults.
- Evaluation of training courses: Written demonstrations of knowledge, such as quizzes, opinion surveys on the usefulness of training, measuring application of knowledge gained in the training course, and impact of the training course on company objectives.
- Management of training courses: Managing the quality of the training program, using feedback to assess future training needs.

## Performance audit for behavior modification

Modifying behaviors can be a long process that requires cooperation and motivation on the part of the person whose behavior needs modifying. One tool that can be particularly useful in behavior modification is to do a performance audit. A performance audit checks the person's behaviors and actions against an established sequence of events or standards, with the aim of developing a score or evaluation of the percentage of positive behaviors. The result of this performance audit can be used to set metrics for improvement, and can serve as a motivator for improvement. It serves as a benchmark to show the current state of behaviors in order to provide the incentive for change.

## First aid

First aid is the first, immediate lifesaving measures given to injured people following an emergency. Employees need first aid training so that they can be prepared for emergencies. Training can be provided on-site by organizations such as the Red Cross, or off-site through community organizations such as colleges, universities, and hospitals. In addition to providing employees access to first aid training, employers also need to provide well-stocked first aid kits. These should be located in visible, accessible locations throughout the workplace. The first aid kit needs to include personal protective equipment such as surgical gloves and mouthpieces to protect anyone administering first aid from bodily fluids. Employers should also post emergency telephone numbers near all telephones in the workplace. They should also post first aid fact sheets to help employees remember the procedures they should follow.

## Building evacuation

OSHA requires companies to have a written plan for evacuating buildings. As part of the plan, exit routes must be clearly marked so people know how to get out of a building even in case of smoke or power outage. In addition, the plan must specify how to communicate the emergency to everyone in the building. This can include both alarms and verbal instructions. Verbal instructions are especially important so that people know that an emergency exists and it is not a drill. The evacuation plan also needs to specify an outside assembly area where employees must gather. Requiring employees to go to a specific area allows safety personnel to ensure that everyone has gotten out of the building safely.

Copyright © Mometrix Media. You have been licensed one copy of this document for personal use only. Any other reproduction or redistribution is strictly prohibited. All rights reserved.

## Sheltering in place

You may need to shelter in place during an emergency rather than evacuating if evacuating is more dangerous than sheltering. For example, if a chemical leak occurs in an area near a workplace, it may be safer for those workers to remain in their building rather than evacuate. An emergency plan should always include procedures for sheltering in place, which needs to include how to do the following:
- Shut down ventilation systems in buildings.
- Shut down elevators.
- Close all exits and entrances, including loading docks and garages, so no one can enter or leave the area.
- Let all building occupants, both workers and visitors, know that an emergency has occurred and what procedures they need to follow.

In addition, the plan should designate which rooms in the building people should gather in: preferably interior rooms with no windows.

## Keeping employees safe from terrorism

Maintaining a secure workplace is one key to keeping employees safe from terrorism. This includes the following: restricting and screening visitors; enforcing parking restrictions; and preventing access to the building through the roof, garages, windows, loading docks, and ventilation systems. Requiring employees and visitors to wear a badge helps security personnel quickly identify unauthorized visitors. Visitors should always sign in and out of the building. Similar procedures should be in place for delivery personnel. In addition to securing the building itself, an anti-terrorism plan also needs to consider the grounds. Clear visibility around the building makes it harder for unauthorized people to approach the building in secret. The grounds should be kept clear of clutter and debris, and trash cans should be either secured to the building or located away from the building.

## Formulating comprehensive emergency/crisis/disaster plans

Developing a comprehensive disaster plan can be accomplished by approaching the task in a planned fashion. First, a cross-functional disaster planning team should be assembled from various functions. The different viewpoints and areas of expertise will serve to strengthen the resulting plan. The next step is for the team to determine the range of disasters that should be planned for; in considering this list, it is important to begin the discussion locally and extend it out regionally and nationally. In addition, the team must consider all types of disasters, including natural, man-made, cybersecurity, and pandemic outbreaks. The team should create an overall disaster response outline, and then this overall scenario should be tailored for each considered disaster to take into account unique requirements. In each case, the team should consider how lines of communication will work, the government agencies that will need to be involved, and any specialized equipment that should be on hand to respond to the crisis. Finally, the team should consider who should be notified of the plan.

### Types of emergencies or disasters to include
When planning for emergency situations, the most important first step is to determine the scope of the business operations, which will guide the preparer to determine the type of emergencies to include. An emergency response plan typically covers emergencies within

- 79 -

Copyright © Mometrix Media. You have been licensed one copy of this document for personal use only. Any other reproduction or redistribution is strictly prohibited. All rights reserved.

the facility, whereas a disaster recovery plan encompasses external disasters that may impact the business. Emergency response plans must take into account the potential for chemical spills or releases, fire emergencies, earthquakes or other natural disasters that may disrupt facility operations, and electrical emergencies (for example, power outages). An emergency response plan should also consider neighboring facilities and their potential to impact facility operations in an emergency situation; for example, if an adjacent facility stores large quantities of a toxic pressurized gas, it is wise to include in your plan a contingency for how the facility will respond if the neighbor has a release.

## On-scene coordinator

The term *on-scene coordinator* comes from the disaster response field and refers to the person on scene at a disaster situation that is in charge of coordinating the various agencies and departments to ensure that all needs are responded to. For example, in a fire disaster, the ranking on-scene coordinator is the fire chief who ensures that medical services and police services are also obtained and apprised of the situation. In a business disaster situation, the on-scene coordinator is generally the emergency coordinator and is a person that is in a position to direct company response resources.

## Planning for site-specific, local, and regional emergencies or disasters

Site-specific emergency response planning should consider resources to be utilized in case the facility's internal production resources or communications networks are affected. Resources that need to be in place to respond to these types of emergencies include communicating with workers and customers about the emergency, ensuring potentially needed experts and contractors are available, and prior identification of key parts or equipment to reduce downtime. Local emergencies are those that involve the local region such as the city or immediate neighborhood. Examples include natural disasters such as floods or tornadoes. Planning for localized disasters should take into account city and county resources, potential disruption of utilities, and fire and police response. Planning for communication with workers should be made. Regional emergencies or disasters are widespread and involve disruption of multiple public agencies, infrastructure, and utilities. Planning for these types of emergencies should include state and federal disaster planning resources.

## Disaster recovery plan

A disaster recovery plan should be led by a Disaster Recovery Coordinator who determines what needs to be done and delegates responsibilities to get the recovery done. A Recovery Team works with the Disaster Recovery Coordinator to analyze and inspect damage, maintain security, repair and restore equipment, and take steps to keep further damage from occurring. The plan may need to include provisions for temporarily relocating the facility while repairs are made. In addition to getting the workplace operational again, a disaster recovery plan should also address assistance employees may need, including financial, medical, and psychological help. Developing a trauma response team to quickly help employees work through their shock and trauma is important. The disaster recovery plan also needs to include communication plans. Employees need to be kept informed about the recovery process, as does the media and outside authorities.

Copyright © Mometrix Media. You have been licensed one copy of this document for personal use only. Any other reproduction or redistribution is strictly prohibited. All rights reserved.

## Potential impact of emergencies or disasters upon business continuity

Emergencies or disasters can be devastating for business continuity. Localized emergencies such as a fire in the facility or even a key piece of processing equipment needing repair can prevent the business from fulfilling its objectives to customers for some period of time. Of particular impact are emergencies that disrupt communications or computer systems or that prevent the company from producing its product. For these reasons, it is important that businesses take time to anticipate potential emergencies they may face and take steps to plan for how they will respond to minimize adverse outcomes that would be costly.

## Identifying relevant external resources

The first step in identifying relevant external resources for emergency and disaster planning is to define the scope of the operation, particularly in regard to its environmental aspects and its personnel structure. When considering environmental aspects, the organization should list its permitted activities (for example, air permits, storm water permits, waste generation activities, hazardous materials storage and use, waste water discharge permits and potential for releases) and should then consider its physical and geographical setting. All of the relevant agencies that grant permits must be part of the external resources identified in the emergency and disaster planning process. In addition, if the site is located near sensitive agricultural or natural resources, agencies overseeing those issues must be considered as relevant external resources. With regard to external resources related to personnel, the organization must consider the number of employees, the demographics of the workforce, and the area resources. The organization must also consider the cultural and language aspects of communication and disaster management to fully account for needed expert resources.

## Accountability, audits, and enforcement in safety management

Management accountability for safety means that managers are responsible for the safety of their workers. Companies can hold managers accountable by making safety part of the supervisor's and manager's performance appraisal, requiring managers to create detailed safety plans, and by creating procedures for measuring the success or failure of safety programs. Audits are one way of measuring the success or failure of a safety program. During a safety audit, independent observers evaluate safety programs, procedures, training, and management and report on areas that need improvement. Enforcement is another tool for safety management. An effective enforcement program includes several components:

- Rules and expectations that are clearly communicated to all workers.
- Training to ensure that all workers understand the rules and know how to do their jobs safely.
- Rewards for correct behavior.
- Consequences for ignoring rules.

## Logical process risk analysis

Logical process risk analysis is a process that helps managers to allocate funds between departments or plants in order to achieve the greatest possible risk deduction. There are six steps involved in this method:

Copyright © Mometrix Media. You have been licensed one copy of this document for personal use only. Any other reproduction or redistribution is strictly prohibited. All rights reserved.

1. Use hazard and control checklists to calculate risk indexes. This will indicate which departments have the highest level of risks. A department with a high risk index has effective controls in place and needs less funding than a department with a low risk index.
2. Determine the relative risk. Rank the departments against each other according to their risk index.
3. Calculate the percent risk index. This number indicates the percent of risk the department contributes to the company's total risk.
4. Calculate the composite exposure dollars. This is the amount of money at risk in the department, including property value, business interruption, and personnel exposure.
5. Calculate a composite risk by dividing the composite exposure dollars by the percent risk index. This gives you the relative risk of the department.
6. Rank departments according to the composite risk in order to see where funds should be allocated.

## Management oversight and risk trees, energy analysis, and fire safety concepts tree

Management oversight and risk trees are tools used to investigate accidents and evaluate safety programs. Elements of an ideal safety program are diagrammed into three levels of relationships: undesirable events, basic events, and criteria. Management oversight and risk trees identify and assess risks and help ensure that errors and omissions are not overlooked. They are useful because they incorporate behavioral, organizational, and analytical sciences to identify risks. Energy analysis analyzes where and how energy is released and transferred in a system. It is useful for identifying hazards in powered machines, equipment, processes, and operations. A fire safety concepts tree analyzes the fire safety of a building to identify deficiencies and corrective actions needed. The tree outlines fire safety objectives and actions needed to achieve those objectives.

## Failure mode and effects analysis

Failure mode and effects analysis analyzes components of a system to see what effect failure of these components would have on the system as a whole. Using a failure mode effects analysis, safety engineers can develop a critical item list to identify failures with unacceptable levels of risk. A failure mode and effects analysis is applicable to a system or manufacturing process. It is a formal process to consider possible failure modes of a system (what could go wrong) and the potential effects (outcomes) if the failure happens. This allows for planning of response to failures that can shorten downtimes and improve overall performance. The first step in conducting the failure mode and effects analysis is to assemble a cross-functional team. Team members to consider are those from operations, maintenance, engineering, environmental health and safety, and accounting. The team then documents potential failures of the system, how likely the failures are, how easy it is to detect the failures, the consequences of the failures, potential root causes of the failures, current control measures in place, additional control measures necessary, and the criticality of the particular failures. The result produces an action list that, when well executed, improves performance.

Copyright © Mometrix Media. You have been licensed one copy of this document for personal use only. Any other reproduction or redistribution is strictly prohibited. All rights reserved.

### Simultaneous timed events plotting analysis and hazard totem poles

Simultaneous timed events plotting analysis analyzes the sequence of events, helping safety engineers visualize complicated events. Hazard totem poles are decision charts that categorize events according to their severity, probability of occurrence, and cost to correct. The ranking helps managers determine which hazards to fix first.

### Safety analysis

Because safety analyses can be expensive and time-consuming, managers need to have a definite purpose for conducting an analysis. One possible purpose for an analysis is to understand how a process works, how components of a process fit together, and what can go wrong in the process. Another reason for doing an analysis is to provide information needed to make decisions and choose a course of action. A third reason for doing an analysis is because the analysis is required by laws, regulations, or contracts. In terms of safety, the ultimate reason for performing an analysis is to prevent accidents by explaining what hazards exist and what controls are needed.

#### Inspections as a form of analysis
Inspections are an approach to preventing accidents. Inspections can be general; this may be a walkthrough that looks at an entire process or system to identify any possible safety problems. Alternatively, inspections can be very detailed, focusing on a specific activity or piece of equipment. Inspections can also be scheduled or unscheduled. Scheduled inspections are performed regularly while unscheduled inspections are random. Inspections should be conducted by people with the training, knowledge, and experience to identify hazards. Inspectors can be coworkers, supervisors, or specialists. Whoever does the inspection needs to be objective and independent so he or she can identify hazards. Inspectors often use checklists to be sure they check everything that needs to be checked.

#### Job safety analysis
A job safety analysis is a formal method used to assess the hazards associated with a job function. They are generally conducted by job title or job classification. The first step in conducting a job safety analysis is to spend time observing people doing the job and develop a list of actions involved in performing the job. For each action or step, the hazards the worker is exposed to must be documented. The job safety analysis must consider the physical hazards, chemical and toxic exposure hazards, potential ergonomic or vibrational hazards, noise exposure hazards, and machinery hazards. The job safety analysis concludes with documented consideration of how each of these hazards are accounted for and controlled.

### Hazard and operability analysis

Hazard and Operability Analysis (HAZOP) is a structured technique to identify hazards of a more systemic or operational nature that can potentially lead to a nonconforming product. It relies on a structured brainstorming technique that guides participants into considering all manner of potential deviations from a process that can lead to failure. The team is assembled and defines the scope or process they will analyze. The brainstorming session then applies guide words to define departures from normal operation that will lead to failure. Potential guide words include *early*, *late*, *more*, *less*, *no*, and *not*. The guide words are used to trigger participants to think of scenarios that represent a deviation; for example,

- 83 -

*Copyright © Mometrix Media. You have been licensed one copy of this document for personal use only. Any other reproduction or redistribution is strictly prohibited. All rights reserved.*

what if a certain step in a process is performed *early*? What are the potential hazards associated with this deviation? The team can use this method to then document deviations from normal processes, possible causes, potential safeguards, potential response options, and who should perform the response action. The result is a robust and well-considered hazard response planning tool.

## Fault tree analysis

A fault tree analysis is a systematic way of analyzing the effects of various faults of a system. It is most useful in analyzing faults in quality or mechanical systems. It uses a logic diagram to document the potential faults in each part of the system. For example, a potential fault of a machine system includes an electrical system failure. One then documents the potential reasons for the potential failure and potential fixes. Each potential reason for the failure leads to another set of reasons, culminating in the fundamental reasons for failure of hardware, software, or human failure.

## Change analysis

Change analysis attempts to analyze and document the effects of a change on a system or organization. The goal is to anticipate all possibly foreseeable ramifications of the change to plan for the communication and tasks associated with executing the change. Some of the elements to be considered include personnel and human resources aspects of the change, permits and regulatory requirements, communication pathways and requirements, both internally and externally, and operational/physical requirements. Change analysis is particularly useful when considering major changes in company structure, mergers and acquisitions, and major product rollouts. In the safety and health arena, the change analysis principles are relevant to implementing requirements for new product lines or new safety requirements that require a multifaceted approach to effectively implement.

## ANSI/AIHA Z10

### Purpose

The purpose of the ANSI/AIHA Z10 is to lay out a framework for an effective occupational health and safety management system. The main elements of the standard require management commitment to the implementation of the standard demonstrated by allocation of resources and attention to its implementation, participation of the organization's employees in the occupational health and safety system, risk assessment, planning of the occupational health and safety system to address the risks identified, followed by evaluation of the system and appropriate corrective action. The system is completed by management review to assess achievement of objectives and adjustment of targets due to newly identified occupational health and safety issues or business objectives.

### Objectives

The main objective of the ANSI/AIHA Z10 American National Standard for Occupational Health and Safety Management Systems is to set a framework for a management system. This systemic approach, while it encompasses compliance as a foundation, seeks to evaluate the organization's risks holistically, and to respond to them in a proactive rather than a reactive manner. The objective is to identify risks before they result in injury or harm, and systematically engage various elements of the organization in planning for risk management. The organization then evaluates its progress and performs root cause analysis

Copyright © Mometrix Media. You have been licensed one copy of this document for personal use only. Any other reproduction or redistribution is strictly prohibited. All rights reserved.

to provide corrective action. This management system serves the overall objective to create a safe workplace that goes beyond compliance.

## Continual improvement

Continual improvement is the foundation upon which the voluntary environmental and occupational health and safety management systems are built. The concept of continual improvement suggests that performance is improved over time, but not always in the same area or at the same pace. The concept also supposes that an organization's performance can never be perfect and that performance can always be improved. For example, the organization can strive to reduce toxic exposures over time by incremental improvements. Incremental improvement is more readily achievable, both financially and on a human scale, than is one big project to make everything perfect. As they say, don't let perfect get in the way of better, since better will be benefiting the workers and the organization on the way to perfect.

## Plan, Do, Check, Act model

Plan, Do, Check, Act is fundamentally important in occupational and environmental health and safety programs. The first step is to Plan—this step involves risk assessment, evaluation of legal obligations, and assessment of stakeholder concerns to guide the organization to create a plan of action and a prioritization of projects to achieve an overall organizational objective. The Do step is the implementation of the plan and the actual carrying out of activities. Concurrently, or at the end of the project, the evaluation of the project's performance is carried out in the Check step. This is a critical part of the cycle and must include measurable criteria that can be used to evaluate a project's success. The results of the evaluation step are used to guide the next iteration of the cycle and lead to the Act piece in response to the assessment of progress.

An example of the Plan, Do, Check, Act cycle is as follows:
The risk assessment revealed that safe lifting behaviors needed improvement to reduce back injuries. A Plan was made to combine education with peer observation and correction to employees' lifting behaviors. This plan was executed in the Do phase of the project. After the project was carried out over time, the Check part consisted of gathering data from the assessments and evaluating whether an observable impact on injuries was made. Based upon the results, the program was modified or Acted upon to improve it.

## ISO 14001 series of environmental management system

<u>Standards</u>
The ISO 14001 series of environmental management standards is a voluntary environmental management system standard that sets a broad framework that any type of organization can use to improve environmental performance. It is a management system that requires commitment from top management to be truly effective. It is up to the organization to assess its environmental aspects and use a ranking process to determine its significant environmental impacts. Those significant environmental impacts are used to guide the establishment of environmental performance objectives. An example objective would be to reduce energy consumption of a processing facility by 10 percent over the next two years. The objective would have a written set of planned activities to achieve the objective, and the organization would periodically assess its progress toward meeting the

- 85 -

Copyright © Mometrix Media. You have been licensed one copy of this document for personal use only. Any other reproduction or redistribution is strictly prohibited. All rights reserved.

objective. Over time, environmental performance (measured environmental impact) is improved with systematic implementation of an ISO 14001 environmental management system.

## Basic elements
The ISO 14001 environmental management system is built upon the Plan, Do, Check, Act model. It requires management commitment for its implementation. The clauses of the standard require that the organization establish an environmental policy, that they commit to compliance with all applicable environmental regulations, that they communicate their environmental programs to employees and make their policy available to the public, that they properly train their employees to do their tasks and to understand their role in the organization's achievement of its environmental objectives, that specific and measurable environmental objectives are established, that the organization maintain document and record control, that the organization conduct periodic internal audits to determine conformance with the standard, and that a system of corrective and preventive actions be implemented. The capstone of the system is the management review process, in which top management periodically review the organization's environmental performance and set objectives and allocate resources for the upcoming year.

## OHSAS 18000 series of occupational health and safety management system

### Standards
The OHSAS 18000 series of occupational health and safety management system standards sets the framework for an effective system to control health and safety risk to workers. The purpose of a management system is to take a systemic approach to the way an organization manages its health and safety function, with the goal of proactively identifying and responding to risk before an accident or an incident occurs. Like all of these standards, the OHSAS standard is built upon the Plan, Do, Check, Act framework, which has proven to be a valuable approach to continual improvement.

### Basic elements
The basic elements of an OHSAS 18000 occupational health and safety management system are as follows:
- Policy: The company sets its policy with regard to occupational health and safety, committing to compliance, communication, and continual improvement.
- Risk Assessment: The company formally examines its operations and the health and safety risks posed by its operations.
- Legal Obligations: The company identifies the legal requirements that apply to its operations and puts into place a mechanism for monitoring changes to these requirements.
- Training: The company enacts relevant training programs to educate workers about occupational health and safety, risks, and how to protect themselves.
- Objectives and Targets; The company sets formal health and safety objectives with measurable targets.
- Communication: Management solicits input from all levels of the organization on health and safety matters, and communicates risks.
- Document Control: Documents associated with the occupational health and safety management system are controlled.

Copyright © Mometrix Media. You have been licensed one copy of this document for personal use only. Any other reproduction or redistribution is strictly prohibited. All rights reserved.

- Corrective and Preventive Actions: A formal process to document corrective actions and perform root cause analyses is instituted.
- Internal Audits: The company internally audits its programs to ensure conformance and as a continual improvement tool.
- Management Review: Top management accepts responsibility for the program and reviews progress toward achieving objectives.

## US Occupational Safety and Health Administration's Voluntary Protection Program

The US Occupational Safety and Health Administration's Voluntary Protection Program is a program that requires a company to systematically improve its health and safety management system in a partnership between the employer and workers. A company must submit an application to OSHA to be admitted in to the program. OSHA conducts a review against established program performance metrics and conducts an on-site review to determine the state of the occupational health and safety management system. OSHA awards employers recognition at two levels of accomplishment: Star and Merit. Star status is awarded to those with a well-functioning system that has opportunities for improvement. Merit status is awarded to those with a robust system of controls and continuous improvement, with participation from all levels of the organization. The overall purpose of the program is to reduce occupational injuries and illnesses and recognize employers with strong occupational safety and health management systems.

## Accident investigation

The primary purpose for investigating accidents is to prevent future accidents from happening. Investigations can also identify causes of accidents and injuries, provide evidence for legal claims and lawsuits, and help assess the amount of loss and damage.

Accident investigation can be expensive, so it is not always possible to investigate every accident. When determining whether to investigate an accident, managers need to consider the following:
- The cost and severity of the accident. Accidents with high losses, whether in life, injury, or property damage, need to be investigated.
- The frequency of the accident. If similar accidents occur frequently, they need to be investigated.
- Public interest in the accident. If the accident affects the community or is otherwise of special interest to the public, it needs to be investigated to provide factual information and protect the company image.
- The potential losses caused by the accident. If the accident may have large losses in life or property damage, it should be investigated.

After an accident, an accident investigation should begin as soon as all emergency steps have been taken to care for the injured parties and to bring the emergency situation under control. Beginning the accident investigation quickly offers several benefits:
- Immediate investigations produce more accurate results because witnesses' memories are fresh and untainted.
- Immediate investigations allow the investigator to study the accident scene itself before it is changed.

Copyright © Mometrix Media. You have been licensed one copy of this document for personal use only. Any other reproduction or redistribution is strictly prohibited. All rights reserved.

- Immediate investigations send a message that the company cares about employees' safety.
- Immediate investigation demonstrates the company's commitment to discovering the cause of the accident and thus preventing future accidents.

Accident investigations should begin as soon as possible. The first tool an accident investigator needs is rope or security tape. Stretching rope or tape around the accident scene will help keep people out of the area, keeping the scene secure, undamaged, and unchanged. Even with rope or tape, though, evidence at accident scenes can dissipate, so the investigator should take photos or a video of the site as soon as possible. Tape measures can be used to mark where items are located and ID tags can be used for marking evidence. Investigators may also need tape recorders to interview witnesses about where they were and what they saw. Particular types of equipment may be needed depending on the type of accident. For example, Geiger counters are needed for radiation releases while colorimeters, sampling equipment, and clean specimen jars are needed for chemical spills.

## Incident reporting system

An effective incident reporting system must have participation of the right people in the organization, which are those people with firsthand knowledge of the incidents being reported. In the case of injuries and near misses, diligent participation of the direct supervisors is most important. They must be properly informed of the type of incidents that need to be reported, exactly what information to report, and how to report it. In addition, the reporters must be given guidance on how the severity of the incident impacts the reporting of the incident. For example, minor incidents such as issuing a bandage for a small cut may need to be only recorded on a first aid log, whereas an injury requiring medical attention must be recorded but also requires notification of the manager on duty so that the insurance reporting and incident investigation process can begin.

A robust incident reporting system that records each incident without fail, and that reports the required information about each incident, can provide valuable information to improve future incident response. Over time, the incident log can be examined for patterns that lead to improved prevention of incidents. For example, temporal investigation may reveal that incidents occur disproportionately on the swing shift or just after break time. Incidents may be more likely to occur in one particular area; discovering these patterns can allow the organization to focus resources on prevention and response in particular areas. Analysis of incident data on leaking equipment, for example, may reveal that a certain piece of machinery develops leaks more frequently than others in the work center; the appropriate response that can be developed from this information is to put that piece of machinery on a more frequent preventative maintenance schedule. The point of tracking incidents and collecting data is to use that data as a continuous improvement tool that provides feedback on performance and guides active response.

## Root cause analysis

Root cause analysis methodology is used to determine the most fundamental reason for a system failure or mistake that has led to an injury or equipment failure. The goal of a root cause analysis is to identify the central cause; this will allow the central cause to be fixed, thereby preventing a recurrence of that particular event. An effective methodology to conduct a root cause analysis is the Five Why method. This method uses around five *why*

- 88 -

Copyright © Mometrix Media. You have been licensed one copy of this document for personal use only. Any other reproduction or redistribution is strictly prohibited. All rights reserved.

questions to determine the root of the problem. An example of a Five Why analysis is as follows:

Q: Why did the valve leak oil? A: The valve had not been replaced.
Q: Why wasn't the valve replaced? A: The workers didn't know it needed to be replaced.
Q: Why didn't the workers know it needed to be replaced? A: No one told them.
Q: Why didn't anyone tell them? A: There is no written replacement schedule available to them.
Q: Why isn't there a written replacement schedule? A: No one has written one.

This process results in an identifiable task that can be undertaken to prevent a recurrence of this problem.

**SWOT analysis**

A SWOT analysis is a tool used to set objectives for an organization or entity. The acronym stands for:

> S = Strengths
> W = Weaknesses
> O = Opportunities
> T = Threats

In a group setting, with participants from all sectors of the organization, the contributors identify the organization's strengths that future moves should capitalize on, the weaknesses that constitute an opportunity for improvement, the opportunities posed by the marketplace, and the threats or competitive disadvantages in the environment. This type of analysis can be used in crisis planning and business continuity planning to determine how the organization can respond to a crisis, and the actions necessary to proactively manage potential crises and turn them into opportunities for advancement.

**Inspection vs. audit**

An inspection refers to checking a list of items that are verifiable. It is narrow in scope and is generally implemented to ensure that regulatory requirements are met. Its objective is to ensure a specific task list has been completed at a predefined frequency. Inspections are also conducted by regulatory agencies to determine permit compliance. An audit refers to a review of an entire management system; its objective is to examine a system designed to manage risk. An audit does not generally examine every document associated with a certain topic, but examines a representative sample to obtain objective evidence of conformance.

**Developing an inspection checklist**

An inspection checklist is developed to meet a specific need to document compliance with a set of objectives. Examples of appropriate objectives for inspection checklists are equipment maintenance inspection checklists or regulatory audit checklists. When developing the checklist, one must define the important elements that need to be checked. In the case of developing a maintenance checklist, one should consult the manufacturer's specifications and product literature to determine the items that need to be checked and at

Copyright © Mometrix Media. You have been licensed one copy of this document for personal use only. Any other reproduction or redistribution is strictly prohibited. All rights reserved.

what frequency. In the case of a regulatory inspection checklist, the requirements of the specific regulation must be consulted to determine the items that need to be checked.

## Developing an audit checklist

The first step in developing an audit checklist is to determine the purpose of the audit. If it is to demonstrate conformance to a third-party certified standard, such as ISO 14001, the standard elements should be considered. In the case of an audit checklist for a management system, a process approach is often beneficial. The audit checklist can be developed for each process to include auditing the elements of the standard relevant to the process. For example, each process will have a training and competence component that should be audited to ensure conformance.

## Planning and executing an audit

The first step in planning an audit is to determine the standard that will be used as a criterion for conformance. This will provide the lead auditor with the scope of the auditing needed. Next, the lead auditor should assess personnel resources to determine how to divide the auditing tasks evenly. For many ISO standards, a valuable audit approach is to audit processes rather than individual elements of the standards. For example, training records and employee competence are assessed in the context of a process rather than as an isolated set of records to be examined. The lead auditor should formulate an audit plan that includes the amount of time dedicated to each audit task, who will be the auditor, and who will be audited. Formal notification in advance should be given to those being audited so they can allocate the necessary time and resources. Any audit findings must be presented within the framework of the clause of the standard being audited. A final written report should then be written, with any findings linked to documented corrective actions.

## Benefits of an effective auditing program

An effective auditing program evaluates the entire management system for potential shortcomings that can adversely impact performance. The audit schedule allows for relatively unrelated departments to evaluate one another's performance and learn from management methods in diverse focus areas of the company. In addition, an effective audit program uses the corrective action system to determine the root cause of inconsistencies uncovered during the audit and provides a feedback tool for continuous improvement. An effective auditing program also allows personnel to receive a measure of cross-training and develop an understanding of how the entire organization functions. This process provides professional development and creates opportunities for learning and advancement.

## Internal vs. external audits

Both internal and external audits provide valuable benefits to an organization. An internal audit provides an opportunity for the organization to perform a self-assessment and determine a measure of performance. Because the organization's employees are familiar with operations, they can perform a more thorough internal audit than can external auditors. However, internal auditors can also develop blind spots resulting from their familiarity with an organization. For example, the organization may not strictly enforce health and safety policies; those that are intimately familiar with the organization may be used to this practice, whereas an external auditor would immediately question the unsafe

Copyright © Mometrix Media. You have been licensed one copy of this document for personal use only. Any other reproduction or redistribution is strictly prohibited. All rights reserved.

practices and produce them as an audit finding. Moreover, an external audit provides an opportunity for the organization to benchmark itself against others in its industry through the findings of an external auditor that has visited other similar facilities.

## Guidelines for quality and/or environmental management systems auditing of ISO 19011

The document "Guidelines for Quality and/or Environmental Management Systems Auditing, ISO 19011" is part of the ISO series of standards, but is not a stand-alone standard to which a company can be certified to. Instead, it sets out best management practices for auditors to use when planning an audit, selecting the audit team, executing the audit, and following up on audit findings. It sets expectations for conducting a quality audit by first defining what the scope of the audit will be and what the audit criteria are. The document then discusses the qualifications of auditors, specifies that the auditors should be independent from the work they are auditing, that audit findings must be grounded in objective evidence, and that auditors must conduct themselves in an ethical and professional manner. The document also discusses the differences between first-, second-, and third-party audits, the responsibilities of the auditor, and the elements that should be included in a well-prepared audit report.

## Methods to document and correct audit findings

All audit findings must be grounded in objective evidence and stated in accordance with the standard being audited to. The auditor must be able to clearly state the evidence evaluated, the finding or conclusion reached, and the element of the standard that has been violated. An example of an acceptable audit finding is as follows: "Four employees were interviewed in the process sampling area and asked whether they were aware of the environmental policy of the company. Two of the employees stated that they knew the policy and where to locate it, whereas the other two were completely unaware of the existence of a policy." To effectively follow up and correct audit findings, they should be grouped into *nonconformances* (areas in which the organization is not conforming to the standard), *areas of concern* (items that are concerning but not yet developed into nonconformances), and *opportunities for improvement* (an extension of best management practices the auditor has observed in other organizations). The management of the findings should be to document them as formal corrective actions that undergo root cause analysis and follow-through of the corrective action.

## Conflict management within a group

Whenever groups of people engage in decision making or change, there is likely to be some kind of conflict. Conflict is not necessarily a negative aspect of group dynamics if it is managed properly and channeled into a positive outcome. In a group endeavor, it is important to first set ground rules for communication and to set expectations for what the group is to accomplish. Appropriate ground rules for communication include the following:
- Each person is entitled to voice his opinion.
- When someone is speaking, other group members must pay attention.
- State whether the group will make decisions based upon consensus or majority rule.
- No put-downs or personal attacks are allowed.

*Copyright © Mometrix Media. You have been licensed one copy of this document for personal use only. Any other reproduction or redistribution is strictly prohibited. All rights reserved.*

Should conflict arise, it is important to stay calm and focused on the actual issue. It is also important for group members to feel that they are being heard and listened to. To convey this, the moderator can use phrases such as "What I hear you saying is…" to be sure that the group understands the various points of view. When people have been given an opportunity to voice their concerns and points of view, the moderator can then seek to define areas of agreement and commonality and, from there, negotiate a path forward to accomplish the group's objectives.

<u>Nonverbal cues signaling conflict or distrust in a group setting</u>
In a group setting, there may be participants that do not agree with the direction the group discussion or decision making is taking, but do not feel comfortable expressing these thoughts outright. However, it is usually quite difficult for people to completely hide their true feelings on a topic if one pays attention to nonverbal cues and body language. Signs of a person's disagreement or conflicting opinion include sitting back away from the group, crossing their arms over their body, rolling their eyes, or even getting up and walking away in the middle of a discussion. People may also divert their attention away from the task at hand by checking their e-mail. When these cues are observed by the group facilitator, it is important to build in opportunities for neutral discussion of a topic and to reengage the participants into the task.

**Team facilitation to achieve desired objectives**

Team facilitation is an important ingredient to ensure that the team achieves its desired objectives. It is important that the team feel comfortable working together and have a basic understanding of each other and the overall objective. The facilitator can use icebreaker activities to allow the team members to get to know one another. This can even be beneficial when the team members know one another, as the icebreaker can be used to allow them to learn something about one another that they don't already know. The facilitator should also do periodic check-ins with the group to provide feedback on how they are progressing toward their objective. Small group activities should be interspersed with whole group activities because some people are more comfortable speaking one-on-one or in smaller groups. Techniques such as using Post-it notes to group ideas into common themes can be used to guide a group toward summarizing what appear to be disparate ideas.

**Refocusing a group discussion**

In group discussions or projects, it is easy for the group to wander off topic or begin discussing a tangential aspect of the task at hand. The facilitator should not take this personally, but should view it as a natural process. There are several techniques that can be used to refocus the discussion:
- Point out the agenda and the time allotted for each task, and make sure the group knows that all of the agenda must be accomplished in the time provided.
- Don't be afraid to say to the group, "That's an interesting idea, but not completely relevant to what we are discussing here," and then refocus the discussion where it left off before the wandering.
- If it's close to a scheduled break time, cut into the discussion and say it's time to take a ten-minute break, and then when everyone reconvenes, the facilitator can refocus the discussion.

Copyright © Mometrix Media. You have been licensed one copy of this document for personal use only. Any other reproduction or redistribution is strictly prohibited. All rights reserved.

- Prepare activities the group can engage in periodically so that the tasks are varied and provide opportunities for different types of learning and interaction. If the group starts to wander off topic, bring out one of the prepared activities to refocus the energy of the group.

## Establishing priorities in a group

Once a team working in a group has done the hard work of brainstorming ideas, it then becomes important to prioritize the ideas into important areas that can be acted upon. No organization will be able to do everything all at once. The following are some methods to rank ideas according to priority:
- Give each person the list of ideas or actions, and ask them to each rank five of them in order of importance to tackle. The ideas that receive the most votes from team members can be ranked and some consensus achieved.
- Set up a simple two-by-two matrix with *How easy to do* on one axis and *How important to do* on the other. Put a dot on the matrix where each idea or task falls; the results can be used to see a visual representation of the relative importance of each task and how difficult it will be to accomplish.

## Using a multidisciplinary team to tackle a complex project

A complex project, by nature, involves many considerations and aspects for a successful completion. It is essential to assemble a multidisciplinary team to ensure that all aspects of the project are carefully considered and accounted for. Each person or group on a multidisciplinary team provides a particular expertise in a project. For example, a new product line will require input from facilities, engineering, sales, accounting, operations/production, and environmental health and safety. Each person on the team will ensure that his or her specialty is accounted for and planned for to ensure nothing is overlooked in the implementation. From a professional development viewpoint, members of the team can learn from one another to broaden their skill set and scope of knowledge.

## Ensuring a multidisciplinary team works together to achieve a common goal

Working with a multidisciplinary team can be a challenge, especially when the team is from very different backgrounds and likely has different issues they believe are important to address. An effective approach to starting out in a positive way is to first hold introductions and to have everyone give a brief discussion of the expertise they bring to the project. Then, it is important that the group as a whole spend some time defining the scope of the project and the desired outcomes. Included in this discussion must be a timeline that states how long the team has to accomplish its goals. Finally, the team needs to set ground rules for their interaction; for example, the team may state that a person cannot be interrupted, or that they will observe time limits on speaking time, or that everyone must be on time, or that people must be fully engaged in the process and not checking their e-mail during the meetings. This type of preliminary work and setting of expectations can get a multidisciplinary team off to a constructive start that enables the various skills and talents to be maximized into more than the sum of its parts.

*Copyright © Mometrix Media. You have been licensed one copy of this document for personal use only. Any other reproduction or redistribution is strictly prohibited. All rights reserved.*

## Effective negotiation process

Negotiation skills are important in many workplace scenarios, not just salary negotiations. There are several elements of an effective negotiation. First, be clear in your own mind about what you'd like to achieve in the negotiation. Put yourself in the other person's position so that you can understand what they want from the negotiation. During the negotiation process, really listen to what they are saying. Validate what they are saying by acknowledging it. Don't be afraid to state what you would like to have the outcome be. Be creative with the proposed solutions to the negotiation; for example, in a salary negotiation, it may be possible to negotiate increased vacation time in lieu of increased salary. Always try to make the outcome of the negotiation a win-win in which each party feels they are getting a fair deal and most of what they want. To that end, it helps to start the negotiation asking for more than you are ultimately willing to settle for. And take your time in the negotiating process and don't be afraid to walk away for a time and come back to it later.

## Planning for and assessing project cost

Effective planning for project costs is an important step in creating the budget for the project, and for ultimately delivering the project on or under budget. To accurately plan for costs, it is important to have all steps and aspects of the project delineated and planned. Unless the project planner has very recent cost information about a certain aspect of the project, it is important to get actual quotes and cost information for the project from potential vendors. It is then important to take into account how far in the future each aspect of the project will occur—if it is more than six months or so, one should factor increases for inflation or vendor price increases, or at least a contingency factor to account for future uncertainties. As the project progresses and actual invoices are received, these must be tracked and referenced back to the project plan to determine whether the project has stayed within its budget.

## Scheduling projects and ensuring deadlines are met

The first step in scheduling a project is to ensure that a full project plan has been assembled that accounts for how long each step of the project will take, and documents which parts of the project must be completed before others can be. The most obvious example is in building a house—one must lay the foundation before the walls can be built and the electrical wiring must be installed before the walls are finished. In a complex project with many deadlines, a large wall calendar or computerized equivalent can be used to graph the project elements according to time and to provide a visual representation of progress. If the various tasks require different contractors or work teams, advance notification of the estimated schedule for their work must be completed. As it gets closer to the time for each contributor to do their part of the project, continued communication on timing is important to ensure that deadlines are met.

## Determining project performance

The criteria used to assess project performance should be determined in advance for each phase and aspect of the project. Common metrics used to assess performance include the following:
- Budget: Is the project at, under, or over budget?

Copyright © Mometrix Media. You have been licensed one copy of this document for personal use only. Any other reproduction or redistribution is strictly prohibited. All rights reserved.

- Time: Has the project or phase been completed on time? If not, how many days overdue is it?
- Quality: Has the work met or exceeded quality standards? For example, has the project passed inspections?
- Conflict: Has the project phase created conflict among the team members?
- Safety: Has the project phase been completed without safety incidents?

**Scope, GANTT chart, and task analysis**

The project scope refers to the objectives and parameters of a particular project. Defining the scope in writing is the first step in project management and allows the project manager to assess the tasks and resources necessary to achieve the objectives. Defining the scope also ensures consideration can be made for necessary permits and personnel that need to be involved in the planning and execution of the project. A GANTT Chart is a project planning tool that graphically represents the project plan in a bar chart format. The tasks necessary to complete a project are listed on the left side of the chart in a column, starting with the first task and proceeding sequentially. The x-axis of the chart represents time. Bars in the chart represent the duration of each task and illustrate the overlapping nature of each task. The GANTT Chart also provides a visual way to show that certain tasks must be accomplished before others. Task analysis refers to a detailed method of defining the varied elements that make up an undertaking and provide a way to document resources that will be necessary in its achievement. It takes into account personnel requirements, tool requirements, documentation requirements, skills necessary (both internal to the organization and external), and how the resources will be provided.

**Timeline, deliverable, and objective**

A project timeline is a description of the various elements of a project according to the order in time in which they will be achieved. The timeline allows the project manager to obtain an overall picture of the time it will take to complete the project. In addition, considering how much time it takes to accomplish the various steps in a project ensures that elements that take longer can be started sooner so that all are accomplished within the project's overall goal. A project deliverable is a tangible work product. Within a complex project, there will be many deliverables by various participants in the project. For example, in a construction project there will be deliverables along the way, such as completion of the project drawings, completion of the project work plan, submittal of the permit applications, and completion of the construction itself in phases. At each point, the deliverable should be a well-defined outcome that can be assessed as part of the project completion.

**Project management techniques**

The occupational health and safety function in an organization touches many aspects and functions of the organization, including operations, maintenance, facilities, administration, human resources, and sales. Many of the projects the occupational health and safety department is involved in will include interaction with some or all of these functions as a team member or team leader. Due to the multidisciplinary teams the health and safety department will be involved in, a basic understanding of project management techniques is important. It is particularly important to understand project planning to ensure all aspects of a project are accounted for, and it is important to understand budgeting and time management to keep projects running smoothly.

*Copyright © Mometrix Media. You have been licensed one copy of this document for personal use only. Any other reproduction or redistribution is strictly prohibited. All rights reserved.*

**Evaluating project specifications to ensure requirements are met**

An essential part of any project plan is to develop specifications or statements of work to ensure requirements are met. The first step in developing the project specification is to understand the scope of the project and what the customer's requirements are (keeping in mind that a customer can be internal or external to the organization). The second step is to understand specifically the permitting and regulatory requirements of the project. This is important in creating the timeline and in determining the project budget and deliverables. For each aspect of the project, a list of expectations and specifications should be created that encompasses the project's physical and regulatory requirements. This will allow periodic assessment of whether the project is on track for timely and proper completion.

**Methods for analyzing cost effectiveness of safety programs**

A cost-benefit analysis compares the cost of expenditures to the benefits achieved through those expenditures. A cost-benefit analysis would be used to determine whether the cost of implementing a safety program is worth the benefits that the safety program will bring. One difficulty in using cost-benefit analysis is determining what value to place on a human life. Return on investment is similar to a cost-benefit analysis. For safety programs, it analyzes whether the investment made to control hazards is returned in the form of lower loss rates and insurance premiums and increased productivity. Cost accounting systems track expenditures related to safety costs. This can include direct costs such as medical and disability payments and indirect costs such as lost productivity, damage to equipment, and wages for overtime or replacement workers.

**Risk**

Risk assessment, risk analysis, risk determination, risk acceptance, and risk characterization
Risk assessment is a general term referring to the process of identifying, analyzing, and evaluating a risk. One approach to assessing a risk involves calculating the cost to correct a hazard and determining if that cost is justified. Risk analysis involves using qualitative and quantitative techniques to measure the potential frequency and severity of a risk. Risk determination identifies risks and estimates their frequency and severity. Risk acceptance means deciding what frequency and severity of risks are acceptable for individuals, companies, and society as a whole. Risk characterization analyzes the effects that exposure to a risk will have on people.

Goals and techniques for identifying risks
The ultimate goal when identifying risks is to identify and describe factors that could lead to illness, injury, accident, or death. One technique used to identify risks is to look at accident histories and try to identify the causes of those accidents. Data from a particular accident can often be generally applied to a process in order to identify risks. Another approach to risk identification is to use systematic and analytical techniques to identify potential losses and risks in a procedure or process. For example, the analysis could compare lists of hazardous conditions against a process or analyze human behavior to see how it is affecting a risk. A third approach to risk identification is to analyze data from accidents. By looking at the frequency and severity of accidents and claims, analysts may be able to identify factors associated with the loss.

Copyright © Mometrix Media. You have been licensed one copy of this document for personal use only. Any other reproduction or redistribution is strictly prohibited. All rights reserved.

Risk management process

The risk management process is a documented way of accounting for *what if*. Risk management attempts to define and document potential risks to the organization, and uses metrics to rank risks in terms of relative importance. The relative risk ranking can be used as a guide to determining which risk can be targeted for improvement first. Risk management is especially important in health and safety, as protecting workers from occupational risks is the foremost consideration of a robust health and safety program. Risk management includes assessing risks from work practices, machinery used, chemicals used, human failures, and workstation design. After identification of risk, the next step is to rank the risks, and then to develop plans for how to eliminate or manage the risks.

Risk ranking methodology

There are many approaches to ranking risks. Most methodologies use a numerical scale (for example, one through five) to indicate how severe or frequent that aspect of the risk is. In the case of health and safety risks, the following are some aspects that should be considered in risk ranking:
- The degree to which the aspect is regulated.
- The potential severity of injury that may result from the aspect not being controlled.
- The number of incidents attributed to the aspect in the past year.
- The degree to which the aspect is controlled.
- The degree of importance of the aspect to stakeholders.
- The amount of time the worker may be exposed to the aspect.

Assigning a number to each risk aspect and totaling them will rank the risks. The final list of ranked risks can be evaluated to determine whether the relative ranking of each risk makes intuitive sense to provide feedback on the risk ranking methodology.

Determining an acceptable level of risk

Risk management and assessment is not a hard science. Many risks are difficult to quantify in likelihood and severity. Organizations must take into account their tolerance for risk to prioritize resources into risk management. Factors to consider include tolerance for potential economic loss, tolerance for adverse publicity that might ensue from incidents, and tolerance for poor employee morale that might ensue from incidents. The organization must also attempt to determine the likelihood of a certain adverse outcome to determine whether minimization of the risk is worth the resources it would take to minimize the risk. The equation of likelihood and severity of risk also involves the business sector the organization is engaged in; for example, a pharmaceutical or medical device company is likely to take fewer risks than a financial services company, based upon the possible consequences of an adverse outcome.

Copyright © Mometrix Media. You have been licensed one copy of this document for personal use only. Any other reproduction or redistribution is strictly prohibited. All rights reserved.

# Practice Test

## Practice Questions

1. The primary danger from biohazards is
   a. sick building syndrome
   b. infection
   c. environmental damage
   d. parasite infestation

2. The best way to deal with hazardous waste is to
   a. eliminate or reduce its production
   b. contain it in a tank, lagoon, or waste pile
   c. treat it through biological, chemical, or physical processes
   d. dispose of it through burial or incineration

3. Teratogens are chemical substances that
   a. cause a fetus to be malformed
   b. produce cancer in humans or animals
   c. change the genetic structure of humans or animals, affecting future generations
   d. displace oxygen, interfering with breathing and oxygen transport

4. "Local" effects from a chemical hazard are effects
   a. from a chemical that damage organs or biological functions
   b. that occur only after repeated exposure to a chemical
   c. that occur after only one exposure to a chemical
   d. from a chemical that injure the skin, eyes, or respiratory system

5. Formerly contaminated air can be recirculated if
   a. it has been cleaned through a system that includes equally efficient primary and secondary systems or a primary system accompanied by a fail-safe monitor
   b. the recirculated air is tested regularly to ensure that it is safe
   c. a process is in place to divert contaminated air outside or shut down the process generating the contaminant if a problem occurs
   d. All of the above

6. How do overcurrent devices help increase electrical safety?
   a. They keep electrical equipment from being turned on.
   b. They interrupt power to electrical equipment if the temperature exceeds a certain level.
   c. They limit the amount of current that flows through a circuit or electrical device.
   d. They restrict access to electrical equipment.

Copyright © Mometrix Media. You have been licensed one copy of this document for personal use only. Any other reproduction or redistribution is strictly prohibited. All rights reserved.

7. Grounding is the process of
    a. equalizing the charge between two conductors that have different charges
    b. removing the charge from two conductors that have different charges
    c. using proper connections to keep conductors in close contact with each other
    d. isolating energized portions of electrical equipment from components people can contact

8. The most dangerous hazard related to cold temperatures is
    a. frostbite
    b. trench foot
    c. chilblains
    d. hypothermia
    e. hives

9. Heat syncope occurs when
    a. blood flows more to the arms and legs and less to the brain
    b. a person working in a hot environment doesn't drink enough water to replace fluids lost to sweat
    c. a person's thermal regulatory system fails, leading to lack of sweating, hot and dry skin, fever, and mental confusion
    d. sweat glands become plugged, leading to inflammation and prickly blisters on the skin

10. Damage caused by ionizing radiation depends on
    a. the tissue and organs exposed to the radiation
    b. the age of the exposed person
    c. the type and dose of the radiation
    d. all of the above

11. Overexposure to microwaves, a source of nonionizing radiation, can lead to
    a. skin aging and skin cancer
    b. inflammation of the cornea
    c. cataracts
    d. skin burns and blisters

12. Dewatering refers to
    a. the process of removing water from an area
    b. any changes made to the moisture content of soil
    c. the process of reducing water content of saturated soil
    d. adding drainage systems to soil

13. Structural failure can be caused by
    a. design errors
    b. changes in material over time because of corrosion, rotting, wear, exposure to sunlight, etc.
    c. physical damage through use and abuse
    d. poor assembly, maintenance, and work habits
    e. all of the above

Copyright © Mometrix Media. You have been licensed one copy of this document for personal use only. Any other reproduction or redistribution is strictly prohibited. All rights reserved.

14. In an explosion, fragment damage is affected by the
    a. force of the explosion
    b. heat of the explosion
    c. length of time the explosion occurs
    d. material involved in the explosion

15. Dust explosions are more likely to occur when
    a. a high concentration of small dust particles are in the air
    b. the air has a high moisture level
    c. inert dust particles are mixed with flammable dust particles in the air
    d. air turbulence is low

16. The most effective means of controlling fire in large buildings is
    a. portable extinguishers located throughout the building
    b. water-based or chemical-based sprinkler systems
    c. heat, smoke, and flame detectors
    d. gas sensors

17. What percentage of workers compensation claims are for lower back injuries?
    a. 10%
    b. 15%
    c. 25%
    d. 40%

18. Recommended Weight Limit (RWL) is defined as the
    a. maximum amount a healthy worker can lift one time without incurring musculoskeletal injuries
    b. weight that healthy workers can lift for up to eight hours without incurring musculoskeletal injuries
    c. weight that materials handling equipment can safely lift and move
    d. weight that healthy workers can move without experiencing physical stress

19. Repetitive strain injuries are caused by
    a. cumulative trauma to tendons, muscles, ligaments, joints, nerves, and other soft tissues
    b. accidents such as slips and falls
    c. improper lifting of a load
    d. lifting of too heavy a load

20. Noise is a hazard in the workplace because it
    a. can lead to temporary or permanent hearing loss
    b. interferes with communication
    c. leads to physiological problems such as high blood pressure
    d. All of the above

21. When testing for air contamination, a grab sample
    a. is a short-term sample of gas or vapor collected with a hand pump or squeeze bulb
    b. is one of a series of samples made as part of a long-term testing program
    c. represents average concentrations of contaminants over a period of time
    d. is not useful for identifying locations of emission sources

Copyright © Mometrix Media. You have been licensed one copy of this document for personal use only. Any other reproduction or redistribution is strictly prohibited. All rights reserved.

22. The maximum level of sound that a human can hear without pain is
    a. 100 dBa
    b. 120 dBa
    c. 140 dBa
    d. 160 dBa

23. When designing a monitoring system, auditory displays are the best choice for messages that
    a. deal with location versus time
    b. do not need to be referred to again
    c. do not require immediate action
    d. are long and complex

24. Machine guards can be used to
    a. keep people or their clothing from coming into contact with hazardous parts of a machine
    b. automatically shut off a machine under hazardous conditions
    c. prevent a machine from being turned on
    d. All of the above

25. Perimeter guards can be used to
    a. stop a worker from pushing two buttons at once
    b. protect a control panel so that normal movement does not activate controls
    c. lock a control so that resistant force, a specific sequence of events, or a key control is needed to activate it
    d. isolate controls from traffic areas

26. Relief valves are used for
    a. gases
    b. liquids
    c. steam
    d. vapor
    e. all of the above

27. In order to be effective, all inspections must be
    a. unscheduled
    b. focused on a specific activity or piece of equipment
    c. conducted by a consultant or specialist brought in from outside the company
    d. conducted by a person with the training, knowledge, and experience to identify hazards

28. Housekeeping is defined as
    a. the process of cleaning an area
    b. putting things away where they belong
    c. ensuring that a facility is clean and germ free
    d. all of the above

Copyright © Mometrix Media. You have been licensed one copy of this document for personal use only. Any other reproduction or redistribution is strictly prohibited. All rights reserved.

29. In order to use color effectively for marking hazards, you should
    a. use bright colors that are easily seen
    b. use any colors as long as you use them consistently
    c. follow the color standards developed by ANSI, OSHA, and the DOT
    d. avoid using colors for marking hazards and relating information

30. The primary purpose of written procedures is to
    a. define an organization's goals, objectives, and principles
    b. provide step-by-step instructions for everyday tasks and emergencies
    c. describe how to implement policies
    d. protect a company from liability

31. What type of eye protection should someone working with lasers use?
    a. No special eye protection is required.
    b. Spectacles with tinted lenses
    c. Safety goggles that can filter the specific wavelength and intensity of the laser beam
    d. Spectacles with side shields

32. Fall protection equipment needs to be used when an employee is
    a. 4 feet above the ground
    b. 6 feet above the ground
    c. 10 feet above the ground
    d. It depends on the industry.

33. Personal protective equipment that can be used to reduce heat stress and thermal injuries include
    a. reflective clothing
    b. gloves
    c. both A. and B.
    d. Personal protective equipment is not suitable for reducing heat stress and thermal injuries.

34. Personal protective equipment should be
    a. the primary means for controlling hazards in the workplace
    b. one part of an overall safety plan
    c. used whenever the employee feels a hazard exists
    d. used in all emergency situations

35. Personal protective equipment needs to be replaced
    a. after every use
    b. when it shows signs of wear, such as cracking, tearing, or holes
    c. on a regular schedule, according to the manufacturer's instructions
    d. It depends on the type of personal protective equipment.

36. Behavior-based safety works best in companies with
    a. a collaborative management style
    b. an autocratic management style
    c. a paternalistic management style
    d. a laissez-faire management style

Copyright © Mometrix Media. You have been licensed one copy of this document for personal use only. Any other reproduction or redistribution is strictly prohibited. All rights reserved.

37. The primary purpose for investigating accidents is to
    a. provide evidence for legal claims and lawsuits
    b. assess the loss and damages
    c. prevent future accidents from occurring
    d. determine the cause of the accident

38. The first tool an accident investigator needs is
    a. a camera or video recorder
    b. a tape recorder
    c. a tape measure
    d. rope or security tape

39. The role of a product safety auditor is to
    a. coordinate safety programs among departments
    b. evaluate the product safety program
    c. evaluate the safety of the product itself
    d. recommend product redesigns and recalls

40. The most effective safety programs are developed
    a. using a collaborative, multidisciplinary approach
    b. by a product safety expert
    c. in accordance with a product safety checklist
    d. by a manager with input from knowledgeable employees

41. In project management terminology, risk is defined as
    a. the probability that an event will occur that will have a negative effect on the project
    b. the possibility of suffering harm or loss
    c. a source of danger
    d. a gamble in hopes of a positive outcome

42. In safety management terminology, risk is defined as
    a. the probability that an event will occur that will have a negative effect on the project
    b. the possibility of suffering harm or loss
    c. a source of danger
    d. a gamble in hopes of a positive outcome

43. Heinrich's incident/injury ratio is
    a. 330:30:1
    b. 300:30:1
    c. 30:10:5
    d. 300:29:1

44. The "prudent man" concept is used to
    a. eliminate or reduce risks
    b. prevent and investigate accidents
    c. determine whether a risk is reasonable
    d. analyze the potential outcomes of a risk

Copyright © Mometrix Media. You have been licensed one copy of this document for personal use only. Any other reproduction or redistribution is strictly prohibited. All rights reserved.

45. A fault tree analysis
    a. seeks to predict human errors by observing employees at work and noting hazards
    b. uses guidewords such as no, less, more, part of, as well as, reverse, and other than to see how a component will behave in unintentional ways
    c. focuses on how frequently an event occurs and how severe the consequences of the event will be
    d. uses symbols to visually display the hazard analysis, creating a logic diagram or flow chart

46. A technic of operations review takes place
    a. after an accident or failure has occurred
    b. before an accident or failure occurs
    c. either before or after an accident
    d. as part of regular inspections and audits

47. ISO 14000 addresses
    a. occupational health and safety management
    b. environmental management
    c. wellness programs
    d. safety and health training

48. In a safety program, return on investment analyzes
    a. whether an investment made to control hazards results in lower loss rates, lower insurance premiums, and higher productivity
    b. the direct and indirect costs associated with safety costs
    c. whether the cost of implementing a safety program is worth the benefits that the safety program will bring
    d. whether a hazard exists and what measures need to be taken to control that hazard

49. The mean is defined as the
    a. number that appears the most times in a series of numbers
    b. distance between the lowest and the highest number in a series of numbers
    c. average number of a series of numbers
    d. middle number in a series of numbers

50. An example of a direct cost related to a loss is
    a. lost productivity due to an injured employee's absence from work
    b. loss of business
    c. loss of reputation
    d. cost to replace damaged property, equipment, or materials

Copyright © Mometrix Media. You have been licensed one copy of this document for personal use only. Any other reproduction or redistribution is strictly prohibited. All rights reserved.

# Answers and Explanations

1. B: The primary danger from biohazards is infection, which occurs when biohazardous agents enter the body or skin through ingestion, inhalation, puncture, or contact.

2. A: The best way to deal with hazardous waste is to eliminate or reduce its production by substituting less hazardous materials or using materials that do not produce hazardous waste. When hazardous materials cannot be eliminated, they must be contained, treated, or disposed of.

3. A: Teratogens are chemical substances that cause a fetus to be malformed. Carcinogens produce cancer in humans or animals; mutagens change the genetic structure of humans or animals, affecting future generations; and asphyxiants displace oxygen, interfering with breathing and oxygen transport.

4. D: "Local" effects from a chemical hazard are effects from a chemical that injure the skin, eyes, or respiratory system. Effects from a chemical that damage organs or biological functions are systemic effects. Chronic exposure refers to effects that occur only after repeated exposure to a chemical, while acute exposure refers to effects that occur after only one exposure to a chemical.

5. D: All of these procedures must be in place in order for formerly contaminated air to be recirculated. The level of contaminants in the recirculated air must be less than the recommended concentrations for health hazards so that there are no potential health consequences for anyone breathing the air.

6. C: Overcurrent devices limit the amount of current that flows through a circuit or electrical device. Fuses and circuit breakers are examples of overcurrent devices.

7. B: Grounding is the process of removing the charge from two conductors that have different charges. Bonding is the process of equalizing the charge between these two conductors.

8. D: The most dangerous hazard related to cold temperatures is hypothermia, which can lead to death if treatment is not given. Hypothermia occurs when a person's body temperature drops below normal. Symptoms include shivering, numbness, and poor judgment. Conscious victims need to be given warm liquids and encouraged to move around. Unconscious victims need to be wrapped warmly and taken for medical treatment.

9. A: Heat syncope occurs when blood flows more to the arms and legs and less to the brain. This heat illness is characterized by fainting in an individual who is not used to a hot environment and has been standing for a long time. The victim needs to lie down in a cool area.

10. D: Damage caused by ionizing radiation depends on all these factors. Infants and children are especially vulnerable to ionizing radiation because their cells are still rapidly developing.

Copyright © Mometrix Media. You have been licensed one copy of this document for personal use only. Any other reproduction or redistribution is strictly prohibited. All rights reserved.

11. C: Overexposure to microwaves can lead to cataracts in the eyes. In addition, microwaves can affect the central nervous system and interfere with cardiac pacemakers.

12. B: Dewatering refers to any changes made to the moisture content of soil. Dewatering changes the volume of the soil and the amount of load the soil can bear.

13. E: All of these factors can lead to structural failure. Types of structural failures include shearing, tension, compression, bending and buckling, and bearing.

14. D: Fragment damage occurs when pieces of material involved in the explosion scatter rapidly through the air. The amount of the scatter depends on the material involved: Glass breaks and scatters easily, whereas tougher materials do not scatter as much but may fly farther.

15. A: Dust explosions are more likely to occur when a high concentration of small dust particles are in the air. Other factors that increase the likelihood of a dust explosion include low moisture content and the presence of oxygen. Turbulence increases the likelihood of an explosion, as it mixes the oxygen and dust particles together.

16. B: The most effective means of controlling fire in large building is a water-based or chemical-based sprinkler system. Fire suppression systems based on carbon dioxide, halons, dry chemicals, and foams are useful for extinguishing fires in areas where water would be hazardous.

17. C: Workers compensation claims for lower back injuries are 25%, related largely to improper lifting, leading to sprain and strain injuries.

18. B: RWL is the weight that healthy workers can lift for up to eight hours without incurring musculoskeletal injuries. It is calculated by multiplying load constant × horizontal multiplier × vertical multiplier × distance multiplier × asymmetric multiplier × frequency multiplier × coupling multiplier.

19. A: Repetitive strain injuries are caused by cumulative trauma to tendons, muscles, ligaments, joints, nerves, and other soft tissues. Such injuries include carpal tunnel syndrome, tendonitis, Raynaud's disease, and fibromyalgia. The hands, arms, neck, and shoulders are most subject to repetitive strain injuries.

20. D: Noise can be a hazard in the workplace for all of these reasons. In addition, noise in the workplace can interfere with learning, cause a startle response, and lead to stress and irritability.

21. A: When testing for air contamination, a grab sample is a short-term sample of gas or vapor collected with a hand pump or squeeze bulb. It is typically used to determine worst-case conditions and to identify the location of emission sources.

22. C: The maximum level of sound that a human can hear without pain is 140 dBa. Work environments must be monitored to ensure that noise levels remain in a safe range. Personal protective equipment such as ear plugs and muffs can protect workers from excessive noise.

Copyright © Mometrix Media. You have been licensed one copy of this document for personal use only. Any other reproduction or redistribution is strictly prohibited. All rights reserved.

23. B: Auditory displays are best for one-time messages that do not need to be referred to again. They are the best choice for short and simple messages that call for immediate action, particularly in work environments where employees are moving around continuously or where it is too bright or dark for visual displays to be easily viewed.

The other option, visual displays, is best suited for long and complex messages that do not call for immediate action; that deal with location rather than time; and that may need to be referenced again later. Visual displays are the best choice for people who work in noisy locations where they might overlook an auditory signal and for people whose jobs require them to remain in the same area or location.

24. D: Different types of machine guards can perform all these functions. For example, power transmission guards can enclose hazardous transmission components so that people cannot come into contact with them, while enclosure guards keep body parts or clothing from contacting the point of operation. Interlocked guards keep a machine from operating when a section is open. Other machine guards can shut off a machine in case of unauthorized access or emergency situations. Machine guards can also be used to prevent flying debris from striking people, muffle noise, capture and enclose dust, and contain and exhaust contaminants.

25. A: Perimeter guards are controls placed between and around push buttons to stop a worker from pushing two buttons at once. All of these options are ways to keep controls from being accidentally activated, such as recessing push buttons and toggles below the surface of a control panel and placing guards over a control to keep it from being pushed accidentally.

26. B: Relief valves are used with liquids. They open when the upstream pressure is higher than a pre-set value, and they close when the pressure returns to normal. Safety valves are similar to relief valves but are used for gas, steam, and vapor.

27. D: Inspections can be scheduled or unscheduled and can be general or specific. An inspection must be conducted by a person with the training, knowledge, and experience to identify hazards. This person may be an employee or an outside consultant.

28. B: Housekeeping means putting things away where they belong. Every piece of equipment and materials should have a designated storage area. The process of cleaning an area (sweeping, wiping surfaces, etc.) is housecleaning, whereas ensuring that the facility is clean and germ free is sanitation.

29. C: In order to use color effectively for marking hazards, you should follow the color standards developed by ANSI, OSHA, and the DOT. Following these standards helps workers remember what the different colors mean so they can quickly understand the warning or hazard being communicated.

30. B: The primary purpose of written procedures is to provide step-by-step instructions for everyday tasks and emergencies. In addition, written procedures can be used to protect a company from liability and to describe how to implement policies (which define an organization's goals, objectives, and principles). To be effective, procedures must be current

Copyright © Mometrix Media. You have been licensed one copy of this document for personal use only. Any other reproduction or redistribution is strictly prohibited. All rights reserved.

and follow a standard format. In addition, workers must be trained in and understand the procedures.

31. C: Someone working with lasers should wear safety goggles that can filter the specific wavelength and intensity of the laser beam being used. The lenses may also be tinted to prevent light damage. Other types of eye protection include spectacles with and without side shields. They can protect the eyes from frontal impact injuries, particles, and splashes.

32. D: It depends on the industry. Different industries have different requirements for wearing fall protection equipment. In a general industry, employees who are more than 4 feet above the ground need to wear such equipment. The number rises to 6 feet for employees in the construction industry and 10 feet for employees on scaffolding equipment.

33. C: Both reflective clothing and gloves can be part of personal protective equipment (PPE) used to reduce heat stress and thermal injuries. Other types of PPE used for this purpose include water-cooled and air-cooled clothing, protective eyewear, and insulated materials.

34. B: Personal protective equipment (PPE) is one part of an overall safety plan. It should not be used as a primary means for controlling hazards because it is always better to remove hazards whenever possible. PPE forms a barrier between the user and the hazard. Its safe and effective use depends on using the right equipment at the right time and using it properly.

35. D: It depends on the type of personal protective equipment. Some types of personal protective equipment (PPE), such as nonwoven hoods and vinyl gloves, are designed to be disposable and should be discarded after use. Other types of PPE, such as rubber and plastic suits, are designed to be cleaned and reused. However, all items of PPE should be inspected regularly and replaced if they show any sign of wear or abrasion. You should also follow manufacturer's guidelines for replacing PPE. Even items that show no sign of wear can have damage or chemical buildup.

36. A: Behavior-based safety is based on the premise that workers who understand and can avoid the behaviors that lead to errors and accidents will have fewer errors and accidents. This approach works best in companies with a collaborative management style because management and workers can work together to evaluate behaviors, analyze accidents, and develop safety plans.

37. C: The primary purpose for investigating accidents is to prevent future accidents from occurring. However, an accident investigation can also provide evidence for lawsuits, indicate the cause of an accident, and help assess the loss and damages.

38. D: The first tool an accident investigator needs is rope or security tape that can be used to cordon off the accident scene. This step will keep the scene intact, preserve evidence, and keep people out of the area. Then the investigator can use other tools, such as the camera or video camera to record the scene, the tape recorder to interview witnesses, and the tape measure to mark where items are located.

39. B: The role of the product safety auditor is to evaluate the product safety program and ensure that it is effective. The product safety auditor reviews documentation, observes

Copyright © Mometrix Media. You have been licensed one copy of this document for personal use only. Any other reproduction or redistribution is strictly prohibited. All rights reserved.

management response to accidents, and makes recommendations for improvements. The auditor may be an outside person or agency or an internal employee who can be objective and autonomous.

40. A: The most effective safety programs are developed using a collaborative, multidisciplinary approach, with people from many different professions working together to identify hazards and develop solutions. Possible members of a team include risk managers, loss control specialists, health specialists, psychologists, and lawyers.

41. A: In project management terminology, risk is defined as the probability that an event will occur that will have a negative effect on the project. Project managers who identify a risk to a project should develop a proactive plan to manage the risk.

42. B: In safety management terminology, risk is defined as the possibility of suffering harm or loss. Risk can be measured by the likelihood that a dangerous situation will occur or by the likely severity of the dangerous situation.

43. D: Heinrich's incident/injury ratio is 300:29:1. This means that of every 330 accidents, 300 result in no injuries, 29 cause minor injuries, and 1 causes a major injury. According to this ratio, a manager typically has many opportunities to improve a safety program before a serious accident occurs.

44. C: The "prudent man" concept is used to determine whether a risk is reasonable. It asks whether it is a reasonable risk for a prudent man. A reasonable risk exists when consumers know and accept the risk and know how to deal with it. An unreasonable risk exists when consumers are unaware of the risk or do not know how to deal with it, or when the risk could be eliminated without making the item overpriced for the market.

45. D: A fault tree analysis uses symbols to visually display the hazard analysis, creating a logic diagram or flow chart. An accident or potential accident is placed at the top of the tree, with lower levels identifying failures or fault events that contributed to the accident. Human error analysis seeks to predict human errors by observing employees at work and noting hazards. Hazard and operability review uses guidewords such as no, less, more, part of, as well as, reverse, and other than to see how a component will behave in unintentional ways. Risk analysis focuses on how frequently an event occurs and how severe the consequences of the event will be.

46. A: A technic of operations review takes place after an accident or failure has occurred. The goal of this review is to identify and prioritize factors that contributed to the accident or failure. As part of its work, the technic of review team can develop strategies for preventing future accidents and failures.

47. B: ISO 14000 addresses environmental management standards. It is a voluntary commitment to environmental protection that includes such steps as developing general requirements and an environmental policy; planning, implementing, and operating environmental programs; checking programs and taking corrective action; and conducting management review of programs.

48. A: In a safety program, return on investment analyzes whether an investment made to control hazards results in lower loss rates, lower insurance premiums, and higher

Copyright © Mometrix Media. You have been licensed one copy of this document for personal use only. Any other reproduction or redistribution is strictly prohibited. All rights reserved.

productivity. Such an analysis is similar to a cost-benefit analysis, which compares the cost of expenditures with the benefits achieved through those expenditures.

49. C: The mean is defined as the average number of a series of numbers. The number that appears the most times in a series of numbers is the mode. The distance between the lowest and the highest number in a series of numbers is the range. The middle number in a series of numbers is the median.

50. D: Cost to replace damaged property, equipment, or materials is an example of a direct cost related to a loss. Direct costs are related directly to an accident. Other examples of direct costs include cost to repair damage to the environment, fines for broken laws and regulations, compensation for injured or ill employees who miss work, payment of medical expenses for injured or ill employees, payments made to survivors in case of the death of an employee, and costs related to the cleanup or investigation of an accident, including travel and legal services. Indirect costs are more intangible but include such factors as lost productivity and lost business.

Copyright © Mometrix Media. You have been licensed one copy of this document for personal use only. Any other reproduction or redistribution is strictly prohibited. All rights reserved.

# Secret Key #1 - Time is Your Greatest Enemy

## Pace Yourself

Wear a watch. At the beginning of the test, check the time (or start a chronometer on your watch to count the minutes), and check the time after every few questions to make sure you are "on schedule."

If you are forced to speed up, do it efficiently. Usually one or more answer choices can be eliminated without too much difficulty. Above all, don't panic. Don't speed up and just begin guessing at random choices. By pacing yourself, and continually monitoring your progress against your watch, you will always know exactly how far ahead or behind you are with your available time. If you find that you are one minute behind on the test, don't skip one question without spending any time on it, just to catch back up. Take 15 fewer seconds on the next four questions, and after four questions you'll have caught back up. Once you catch back up, you can continue working each problem at your normal pace.

Furthermore, don't dwell on the problems that you were rushed on. If a problem was taking up too much time and you made a hurried guess, it must be difficult. The difficult questions are the ones you are most likely to miss anyway, so it isn't a big loss. It is better to end with more time than you need than to run out of time.

Lastly, sometimes it is beneficial to slow down if you are constantly getting ahead of time. You are always more likely to catch a careless mistake by working more slowly than quickly, and among very high-scoring test takers (those who are likely to have lots of time left over), careless errors affect the score more than mastery of material.

# Secret Key #2 - Guessing is not Guesswork

You probably know that guessing is a good idea. Unlike other standardized tests, there is no penalty for getting a wrong answer. Even if you have no idea about a question, you still have a 20-25% chance of getting it right.

Most test takers do not understand the impact that proper guessing can have on their score. Unless you score extremely high, guessing will significantly contribute to your final score.

## Monkeys Take the Test

What most test takers don't realize is that to insure that 20-25% chance, you have to guess randomly. If you put 20 monkeys in a room to take this test, assuming they answered once per question and behaved themselves, on average they would get 20-25% of the questions correct. Put 20 test takers in the room, and the average will be much lower among guessed questions. Why?
   1. The test writers intentionally write deceptive answer choices that "look" right. A test

Copyright © Mometrix Media. You have been licensed one copy of this document for personal use only. Any other reproduction or redistribution is strictly prohibited. All rights reserved.

taker has no idea about a question, so he picks the "best looking" answer, which is often wrong. The monkey has no idea what looks good and what doesn't, so it will consistently be right about 20-25% of the time.

2. Test takers will eliminate answer choices from the guessing pool based on a hunch or intuition. Simple but correct answers often get excluded, leaving a 0% chance of being correct. The monkey has no clue, and often gets lucky with the best choice.

This is why the process of elimination endorsed by most test courses is flawed and detrimental to your performance. Test takers don't guess; they make an ignorant stab in the dark that is usually worse than random.

# $5 Challenge

Let me introduce one of the most valuable ideas of this course—the $5 challenge:

*You only mark your "best guess" if you are willing to bet $5 on it.*
*You only eliminate choices from guessing if you are willing to bet $5 on it.*

Why $5? Five dollars is an amount of money that is small yet not insignificant, and can really add up fast (20 questions could cost you $100). Likewise, each answer choice on one question of the test will have a small impact on your overall score, but it can really add up to a lot of points in the end.

The process of elimination IS valuable. The following shows your chance of guessing it right:

| If you eliminate wrong answer choices until only this many remain: | Chance of getting it correct: |
|---|---|
| 1 | 100% |
| 2 | 50% |
| 3 | 33% |

However, if you accidentally eliminate the right answer or go on a hunch for an incorrect answer, your chances drop dramatically—to 0%. By guessing among all the answer choices, you are GUARANTEED to have a shot at the right answer.

That's why the $5 test is so valuable. If you give up the advantage and safety of a pure guess, it had better be worth the risk.

What we still haven't covered is how to be sure that whatever guess you make is truly random. Here's the easiest way:

*Always pick the first answer choice among those remaining.*

Such a technique means that you have decided, **before you see a single test question,** exactly how you are going to guess, and since the order of choices tells you nothing about which one is correct, this guessing technique is perfectly random.

Copyright © Mometrix Media. You have been licensed one copy of this document for personal use only. Any other reproduction or redistribution is strictly prohibited. All rights reserved.

This section is not meant to scare you away from making educated guesses or eliminating choices; you just need to define when a choice is worth eliminating. The $5 test, along with a pre-defined random guessing strategy, is the best way to make sure you reap all of the benefits of guessing.

# Secret Key #3 - Practice Smarter, Not Harder

Many test takers delay the test preparation process because they dread the awful amounts of practice time they think necessary to succeed on the test. We have refined an effective method that will take you only a fraction of the time.

There are a number of "obstacles" in the path to success. Among these are answering questions, finishing in time, and mastering test-taking strategies. All must be executed on the day of the test at peak performance, or your score will suffer. The test is a mental marathon that has a large impact on your future.

Just like a marathon runner, it is important to work your way up to the full challenge. So first you just worry about questions, and then time, and finally strategy:

## Success Strategy

1. Find a good source for practice tests.
2. If you are willing to make a larger time investment, consider using more than one study guide. Often the different approaches of multiple authors will help you "get" difficult concepts.
3. Take a practice test with no time constraints, with all study helps, "open book." Take your time with questions and focus on applying strategies.
4. Take a practice test with time constraints, with all guides, "open book."
5. Take a final practice test without open material and with time limits.

If you have time to take more practice tests, just repeat step 5. By gradually exposing yourself to the full rigors of the test environment, you will condition your mind to the stress of test day and maximize your success.

# Secret Key #4 - **Prepare, Don't Procrastinate**

Let me state an obvious fact: if you take the test three times, you will probably get three different scores. This is due to the way you feel on test day, the level of preparedness you have, and the version of the test you see. Despite the test writers' claims to the contrary, some versions of the test WILL be easier for you than others.

Since your future depends so much on your score, you should maximize your chances of success. In order to maximize the likelihood of success, you've got to prepare in advance.

Copyright © Mometrix Media. You have been licensed one copy of this document for personal use only. Any other reproduction or redistribution is strictly prohibited. All rights reserved.

This means taking practice tests and spending time learning the information and test taking strategies you will need to succeed.

Never go take the actual test as a "practice" test, expecting that you can just take it again if you need to. Take all the practice tests you can on your own, but when you go to take the official test, be prepared, be focused, and do your best the first time!

# Secret Key #5 - Test Yourself

Everyone knows that time is money. There is no need to spend too much of your time or too little of your time preparing for the test. You should only spend as much of your precious time preparing as is necessary for you to get the score you need.

Once you have taken a practice test under real conditions of time constraints, then you will know if you are ready for the test or not.

If you have scored extremely high the first time that you take the practice test, then there is not much point in spending countless hours studying. You are already there.

Benchmark your abilities by retaking practice tests and seeing how much you have improved. Once you consistently score high enough to guarantee success, then you are ready.

If you have scored well below where you need, then knuckle down and begin studying in earnest. Check your improvement regularly through the use of practice tests under real conditions. Above all, don't worry, panic, or give up. The key is perseverance!

Then, when you go to take the test, remain confident and remember how well you did on the practice tests. If you can score high enough on a practice test, then you can do the same on the real thing.

# General Strategies

The most important thing you can do is to ignore your fears and jump into the test immediately. Do not be overwhelmed by any strange-sounding terms. You have to jump into the test like jumping into a pool—all at once is the easiest way.

## Make Predictions

As you read and understand the question, try to guess what the answer will be. Remember that several of the answer choices are wrong, and once you begin reading them, your mind will immediately become cluttered with answer choices designed to throw you off. Your mind is typically the most focused immediately after you have read the question and digested its contents. If you can, try to predict what the correct answer will be. You may be surprised at what you can predict.

Copyright © Mometrix Media. You have been licensed one copy of this document for personal use only. Any other reproduction or redistribution is strictly prohibited. All rights reserved.

Quickly scan the choices and see if your prediction is in the listed answer choices. If it is, then you can be quite confident that you have the right answer. It still won't hurt to check the other answer choices, but most of the time, you've got it!

## Answer the Question

It may seem obvious to only pick answer choices that answer the question, but the test writers can create some excellent answer choices that are wrong. Don't pick an answer just because it sounds right, or you believe it to be true. It MUST answer the question. Once you've made your selection, always go back and check it against the question and make sure that you didn't misread the question and that the answer choice does answer the question posed.

## Benchmark

After you read the first answer choice, decide if you think it sounds correct or not. If it doesn't, move on to the next answer choice. If it does, mentally mark that answer choice. This doesn't mean that you've definitely selected it as your answer choice, it just means that it's the best you've seen thus far. Go ahead and read the next choice. If the next choice is worse than the one you've already selected, keep going to the next answer choice. If the next choice is better than the choice you've already selected, mentally mark the new answer choice as your best guess.

The first answer choice that you select becomes your standard. Every other answer choice must be benchmarked against that standard. That choice is correct until proven otherwise by another answer choice beating it out. Once you've decided that no other answer choice seems as good, do one final check to ensure that your answer choice answers the question posed.

## Valid Information

Don't discount any of the information provided in the question. Every piece of information may be necessary to determine the correct answer. None of the information in the question is there to throw you off (while the answer choices will certainly have information to throw you off). If two seemingly unrelated topics are discussed, don't ignore either. You can be confident there is a relationship, or it wouldn't be included in the question, and you are probably going to have to determine what is that relationship to find the answer.

## Avoid "Fact Traps"

Don't get distracted by a choice that is factually true. Your search is for the answer that answers the question. Stay focused and don't fall for an answer that is true but irrelevant. Always go back to the question and make sure you're choosing an answer that actually answers the question and is not just a true statement. An answer can be factually correct, but it MUST answer the question asked. Additionally, two answers can both be seemingly correct, so be sure to read all of the answer choices, and make sure that you get the one that BEST answers the question.

## Milk the Question

Some of the questions may throw you completely off. They might deal with a subject you have not been exposed to, or one that you haven't reviewed in years. While your lack of knowledge about the subject will be a hindrance, the question itself can give you many clues that will help you find the correct answer. Read the question carefully and look for clues. Watch particularly for adjectives and nouns describing difficult terms or words that you

Copyright © Mometrix Media. You have been licensed one copy of this document for personal use only. Any other reproduction or redistribution is strictly prohibited. All rights reserved.

don't recognize. Regardless of whether you completely understand a word or not, replacing it with a synonym, either provided or one you more familiar with, may help you to understand what the questions are asking. Rather than wracking your mind about specific detailed information concerning a difficult term or word, try to use mental substitutes that are easier to understand.

## The Trap of Familiarity

Don't just choose a word because you recognize it. On difficult questions, you may not recognize a number of words in the answer choices. The test writers don't put "make-believe" words on the test, so don't think that just because you only recognize all the words in one answer choice that that answer choice must be correct. If you only recognize words in one answer choice, then focus on that one. Is it correct? Try your best to determine if it is correct. If it is, that's great. If not, eliminate it. Each word and answer choice you eliminate increases your chances of getting the question correct, even if you then have to guess among the unfamiliar choices.

## Eliminate Answers

Eliminate choices as soon as you realize they are wrong. But be careful! Make sure you consider all of the possible answer choices. Just because one appears right, doesn't mean that the next one won't be even better! The test writers will usually put more than one good answer choice for every question, so read all of them. Don't worry if you are stuck between two that seem right. By getting down to just two remaining possible choices, your odds are now 50/50. Rather than wasting too much time, play the odds. You are guessing, but guessing wisely because you've been able to knock out some of the answer choices that you know are wrong. If you are eliminating choices and realize that the last answer choice you are left with is also obviously wrong, don't panic. Start over and consider each choice again. There may easily be something that you missed the first time and will realize on the second pass.

## Tough Questions

If you are stumped on a problem or it appears too hard or too difficult, don't waste time. Move on! Remember though, if you can quickly check for obviously incorrect answer choices, your chances of guessing correctly are greatly improved. Before you completely give up, at least try to knock out a couple of possible answers. Eliminate what you can and then guess at the remaining answer choices before moving on.

## Brainstorm

If you get stuck on a difficult question, spend a few seconds quickly brainstorming. Run through the complete list of possible answer choices. Look at each choice and ask yourself, "Could this answer the question satisfactorily?" Go through each answer choice and consider it independently of the others. By systematically going through all possibilities, you may find something that you would otherwise overlook. Remember though that when you get stuck, it's important to try to keep moving.

## Read Carefully

Understand the problem. Read the question and answer choices carefully. Don't miss the question because you misread the terms. You have plenty of time to read each question thoroughly and make sure you understand what is being asked. Yet a happy medium must be attained, so don't waste too much time. You must read carefully, but efficiently.

Copyright © Mometrix Media. You have been licensed one copy of this document for personal use only. Any other reproduction or redistribution is strictly prohibited. All rights reserved.

## Face Value

When in doubt, use common sense. Always accept the situation in the problem at face value. Don't read too much into it. These problems will not require you to make huge leaps of logic. The test writers aren't trying to throw you off with a cheap trick. If you have to go beyond creativity and make a leap of logic in order to have an answer choice answer the question, then you should look at the other answer choices. Don't overcomplicate the problem by creating theoretical relationships or explanations that will warp time or space. These are normal problems rooted in reality. It's just that the applicable relationship or explanation may not be readily apparent and you have to figure things out. Use your common sense to interpret anything that isn't clear.

## Prefixes

If you're having trouble with a word in the question or answer choices, try dissecting it. Take advantage of every clue that the word might include. Prefixes and suffixes can be a huge help. Usually they allow you to determine a basic meaning. Pre- means before, post- means after, pro - is positive, de- is negative. From these prefixes and suffixes, you can get an idea of the general meaning of the word and try to put it into context. Beware though of any traps. Just because con- is the opposite of pro-, doesn't necessarily mean congress is the opposite of progress!

## Hedge Phrases

Watch out for critical hedge phrases, led off with words such as "likely," "may," "can," "sometimes," "often," "almost," "mostly," "usually," "generally," "rarely," and "sometimes." Question writers insert these hedge phrases to cover every possibility. Often an answer choice will be wrong simply because it leaves no room for exception. Unless the situation calls for them, avoid answer choices that have definitive words like "exactly," and "always."

## Switchback Words

Stay alert for "switchbacks." These are the words and phrases frequently used to alert you to shifts in thought. The most common switchback word is "but." Others include "although," "however," "nevertheless," "on the other hand," "even though," "while," "in spite of," "despite," and "regardless of."

## New Information

Correct answer choices will rarely have completely new information included. Answer choices typically are straightforward reflections of the material asked about and will directly relate to the question. If a new piece of information is included in an answer choice that doesn't even seem to relate to the topic being asked about, then that answer choice is likely incorrect. All of the information needed to answer the question is usually provided for you in the question. You should not have to make guesses that are unsupported or choose answer choices that require unknown information that cannot be reasoned from what is given.

## Time Management

On technical questions, don't get lost on the technical terms. Don't spend too much time on any one question. If you don't know what a term means, then odds are you aren't going to get much further since you don't have a dictionary. You should be able to immediately recognize whether or not you know a term. If you don't, work with the other clues that you have—the other answer choices and terms provided—but don't waste too much time trying

*Copyright © Mometrix Media. You have been licensed one copy of this document for personal use only. Any other reproduction or redistribution is strictly prohibited. All rights reserved.*

to figure out a difficult term that you don't know.

## Contextual Clues

Look for contextual clues. An answer can be right but not the correct answer. The contextual clues will help you find the answer that is most right and is correct. Understand the context in which a phrase or statement is made. This will help you make important distinctions.

## Don't Panic

Panicking will not answer any questions for you; therefore, it isn't helpful. When you first see the question, if your mind goes blank, take a deep breath. Force yourself to mechanically go through the steps of solving the problem using the strategies you've learned.

## Pace Yourself

Don't get clock fever. It's easy to be overwhelmed when you're looking at a page full of questions, your mind is full of random thoughts and feeling confused, and the clock is ticking down faster than you would like. Calm down and maintain the pace that you have set for yourself. As long as you are on track by monitoring your pace, you are guaranteed to have enough time for yourself. When you get to the last few minutes of the test, it may seem like you won't have enough time left, but if you only have as many questions as you should have left at that point, then you're right on track!

## Answer Selection

The best way to pick an answer choice is to eliminate all of those that are wrong, until only one is left and confirm that is the correct answer. Sometimes though, an answer choice may immediately look right. Be careful! Take a second to make sure that the other choices are not equally obvious. Don't make a hasty mistake. There are only two times that you should stop before checking other answers. First is when you are positive that the answer choice you have selected is correct. Second is when time is almost out and you have to make a quick guess!

## Check Your Work

Since you will probably not know every term listed and the answer to every question, it is important that you get credit for the ones that you do know. Don't miss any questions through careless mistakes. If at all possible, try to take a second to look back over your answer selection and make sure you've selected the correct answer choice and haven't made a costly careless mistake (such as marking an answer choice that you didn't mean to mark). The time it takes for this quick double check should more than pay for itself in caught mistakes.

## Beware of Directly Quoted Answers

Sometimes an answer choice will repeat word for word a portion of the question or reference section. However, beware of such exact duplication. It may be a trap! More than likely, the correct choice will paraphrase or summarize a point, rather than being exactly the same wording.

Copyright © Mometrix Media. You have been licensed one copy of this document for personal use only. Any other reproduction or redistribution is strictly prohibited. All rights reserved.

## Slang

Scientific sounding answers are better than slang ones. An answer choice that begins "To compare the outcomes…" is much more likely to be correct than one that begins "Because some people insisted…"

## Extreme Statements

Avoid wild answers that throw out highly controversial ideas that are proclaimed as established fact. An answer choice that states the "process should used in certain situations, if…" is much more likely to be correct than one that states the "process should be discontinued completely." The first is a calm rational statement and doesn't even make a definitive, uncompromising stance, using a hedge word "if" to provide wiggle room, whereas the second choice is a radical idea and far more extreme.

## Answer Choice Families

When you have two or more answer choices that are direct opposites or parallels, one of them is usually the correct answer. For instance, if one answer choice states "x increases" and another answer choice states "x decreases" or "y increases," then those two or three answer choices are very similar in construction and fall into the same family of answer choices. A family of answer choices consists of two or three answer choices, very similar in construction, but often with directly opposite meanings. Usually the correct answer choice will be in that family of answer choices. The "odd man out" or answer choice that doesn't seem to fit the parallel construction of the other answer choices is more likely to be incorrect.

Copyright © Mometrix Media. You have been licensed one copy of this document for personal use only. Any other reproduction or redistribution is strictly prohibited. All rights reserved.

# Special Report: How to Overcome Test Anxiety

The very nature of tests caters to some level of anxiety, nervousness, or tension, just as we feel for any important event that occurs in our lives. A little bit of anxiety or nervousness can be a good thing. It helps us with motivation, and makes achievement just that much sweeter. However, too much anxiety can be a problem, especially if it hinders our ability to function and perform.

"Test anxiety," is the term that refers to the emotional reactions that some test-takers experience when faced with a test or exam. Having a fear of testing and exams is based upon a rational fear, since the test-taker's performance can shape the course of an academic career. Nevertheless, experiencing excessive fear of examinations will only interfere with the test-taker's ability to perform and chance to be successful.

There are a large variety of causes that can contribute to the development and sensation of test anxiety. These include, but are not limited to, lack of preparation and worrying about issues surrounding the test.

## Lack of Preparation

Lack of preparation can be identified by the following behaviors or situations:

Not scheduling enough time to study, and therefore cramming the night before the test or exam
Managing time poorly, to create the sensation that there is not enough time to do everything
Failing to organize the text information in advance, so that the study material consists of the entire text and not simply the pertinent information
Poor overall studying habits

Worrying, on the other hand, can be related to both the test taker, or many other factors around him/her that will be affected by the results of the test. These include worrying about:

Previous performances on similar exams, or exams in general
How friends and other students are achieving
The negative consequences that will result from a poor grade or failure

There are three primary elements to test anxiety. Physical components, which involve the same typical bodily reactions as those to acute anxiety (to be discussed below). Emotional factors have to do with fear or panic. Mental or cognitive issues concerning attention spans and memory abilities.

Copyright © Mometrix Media. You have been licensed one copy of this document for personal use only. Any other reproduction or redistribution is strictly prohibited. All rights reserved.

# Physical Signals

There are many different symptoms of test anxiety, and these are not limited to mental and emotional strain. Frequently there are a range of physical signals that will let a test taker know that he/she is suffering from test anxiety. These bodily changes can include the following:

Perspiring
Sweaty palms
Wet, trembling hands
Nausea
Dry mouth
A knot in the stomach
Headache
Faintness
Muscle tension
Aching shoulders, back and neck
Rapid heart beat
Feeling too hot/cold

To recognize the sensation of test anxiety, a test-taker should monitor him/herself for the following sensations:

The physical distress symptoms as listed above
Emotional sensitivity, expressing emotional feelings such as the need to cry or laugh too much, or a sensation of anger or helplessness
A decreased ability to think, causing the test-taker to blank out or have racing thoughts that are hard to organize or control.

Though most students will feel some level of anxiety when faced with a test or exam, the majority can cope with that anxiety and maintain it at a manageable level. However, those who cannot are faced with a very real and very serious condition, which can and should be controlled for the immeasurable benefit of this sufferer.

Naturally, these sensations lead to negative results for the testing experience. The most common effects of test anxiety have to do with nervousness and mental blocking.

# Nervousness

Nervousness can appear in several different levels:

The test-taker's difficulty, or even inability to read and understand the questions on the test
The difficulty or inability to organize thoughts to a coherent form
The difficulty or inability to recall key words and concepts relating to the testing questions (especially essays)
The receipt of poor grades on a test, though the test material was well known by the test taker

Copyright © Mometrix Media. You have been licensed one copy of this document for personal use only. Any other reproduction or redistribution is strictly prohibited. All rights reserved.

Conversely, a person may also experience mental blocking, which involves:

Blanking out on test questions
Only remembering the correct answers to the questions when the test has already finished.

Fortunately for test anxiety sufferers, beating these feelings, to a large degree, has to do with proper preparation. When a test taker has a feeling of preparedness, then anxiety will be dramatically lessened.

The first step to resolving anxiety issues is to distinguish which of the two types of anxiety are being suffered. If the anxiety is a direct result of a lack of preparation, this should be considered a normal reaction, and the anxiety level (as opposed to the test results) shouldn't be anything to worry about. However, if, when adequately prepared, the test-taker still panics, blanks out, or seems to overreact, this is not a fully rational reaction. While this can be considered normal too, there are many ways to combat and overcome these effects.

Remember that anxiety cannot be entirely eliminated, however, there are ways to minimize it, to make the anxiety easier to manage. Preparation is one of the best ways to minimize test anxiety. Therefore the following techniques are wise in order to best fight off any anxiety that may want to build.

To begin with, try to avoid cramming before a test, whenever it is possible. By trying to memorize an entire term's worth of information in one day, you'll be shocking your system, and not giving yourself a very good chance to absorb the information. This is an easy path to anxiety, so for those who suffer from test anxiety, cramming should not even be considered an option.

Instead of cramming, work throughout the semester to combine all of the material which is presented throughout the semester, and work on it gradually as the course goes by, making sure to master the main concepts first, leaving minor details for a week or so before the test.

To study for the upcoming exam, be sure to pose questions that may be on the examination, to gauge the ability to answer them by integrating the ideas from your texts, notes and lectures, as well as any supplementary readings.

If it is truly impossible to cover all of the information that was covered in that particular term, concentrate on the most important portions, that can be covered very well. Learn these concepts as best as possible, so that when the test comes, a goal can be made to use these concepts as presentations of your knowledge.

In addition to study habits, changes in attitude are critical to beating a struggle with test anxiety. In fact, an improvement of the perspective over the entire test-taking experience can actually help a test taker to enjoy studying and therefore improve the overall experience. Be certain not to overemphasize the significance of the grade - know that the result of the test is neither a reflection of self worth, nor is it a measure of intelligence; one grade will not predict a person's future success.

Copyright © Mometrix Media. You have been licensed one copy of this document for personal use only. Any other reproduction or redistribution is strictly prohibited. All rights reserved.

To improve an overall testing outlook, the following steps should be tried:

Keeping in mind that the most reasonable expectation for taking a test is to expect to try to demonstrate as much of what you know as you possibly can.
Reminding ourselves that a test is only one test; this is not the only one, and there will be others.
The thought of thinking of oneself in an irrational, all-or-nothing term should be avoided at all costs.
A reward should be designated for after the test, so there's something to look forward to. Whether it be going to a movie, going out to eat, or simply visiting friends, schedule it in advance, and do it no matter what result is expected on the exam.

Test-takers should also keep in mind that the basics are some of the most important things, even beyond anti-anxiety techniques and studying. Never neglect the basic social, emotional and biological needs, in order to try to absorb information. In order to best achieve, these three factors must be held as just as important as the studying itself.

## Study Steps

Remember the following important steps for studying:

Maintain healthy nutrition and exercise habits. Continue both your recreational activities and social pass times. These both contribute to your physical and emotional well being.
Be certain to get a good amount of sleep, especially the night before the test, because when you're overtired you are not able to perform to the best of your best ability.
Keep the studying pace to a moderate level by taking breaks when they are needed, and varying the work whenever possible, to keep the mind fresh instead of getting bored. When enough studying has been done that all the material that can be learned has been learned, and the test taker is prepared for the test, stop studying and do something relaxing such as listening to music, watching a movie, or taking a warm bubble bath.

There are also many other techniques to minimize the uneasiness or apprehension that is experienced along with test anxiety before, during, or even after the examination. In fact, there are a great deal of things that can be done to stop anxiety from interfering with lifestyle and performance. Again, remember that anxiety will not be eliminated entirely, and it shouldn't be. Otherwise that "up" feeling for exams would not exist, and most of us depend on that sensation to perform better than usual. However, this anxiety has to be at a level that is manageable.

Of course, as we have just discussed, being prepared for the exam is half the battle right away. Attending all classes, finding out what knowledge will be expected on the exam, and knowing the exam schedules are easy steps to lowering anxiety. Keeping up with work will remove the need to cram, and efficient study habits will eliminate wasted time. Studying should be done in an ideal location for concentration, so that it is simple to become interested in the material and give it complete attention. A method such as SQ3R (Survey, Question, Read, Recite, Review) is a wonderful key to follow to make sure that the study habits are as effective as possible, especially in the case of learning from a

Copyright © Mometrix Media. You have been licensed one copy of this document for personal use only. Any other reproduction or redistribution is strictly prohibited. All rights reserved.

textbook. Flashcards are great techniques for memorization. Learning to take good notes will mean that notes will be full of useful information, so that less sifting will need to be done to seek out what is pertinent for studying. Reviewing notes after class and then again on occasion will keep the information fresh in the mind. From notes that have been taken summary sheets and outlines can be made for simpler reviewing.

A study group can also be a very motivational and helpful place to study, as there will be a sharing of ideas, all of the minds can work together, to make sure that everyone understands, and the studying will be made more interesting because it will be a social occasion.

Basically, though, as long as the test-taker remains organized and self confident, with efficient study habits, less time will need to be spent studying, and higher grades will be achieved.

To become self confident, there are many useful steps. The first of these is "self talk." It has been shown through extensive research, that self-talk for students who suffer from test anxiety, should be well monitored, in order to make sure that it contributes to self confidence as opposed to sinking the student. Frequently the self talk of test-anxious students is negative or self-defeating, thinking that everyone else is smarter and faster, that they always mess up, and that if they don't do well, they'll fail the entire course. It is important to decreasing anxiety that awareness is made of self talk. Try writing any negative self thoughts and then disputing them with a positive statement instead. Begin self-encouragement as though it was a friend speaking. Repeat positive statements to help reprogram the mind to believing in successes instead of failures.

## Helpful Techniques

Other extremely helpful techniques include:

Self-visualization of doing well and reaching goals
While aiming for an "A" level of understanding, don't try to "overprotect" by setting your expectations lower. This will only convince the mind to stop studying in order to meet the lower expectations.
Don't make comparisons with the results or habits of other students. These are individual factors, and different things work for different people, causing different results.
Strive to become an expert in learning what works well, and what can be done in order to improve. Consider collecting this data in a journal.
Create rewards for after studying instead of doing things before studying that will only turn into avoidance behaviors.
Make a practice of relaxing - by using methods such as progressive relaxation, self-hypnosis, guided imagery, etc - in order to make relaxation an automatic sensation.
Work on creating a state of relaxed concentration so that concentrating will take on the focus of the mind, so that none will be wasted on worrying.
Take good care of the physical self by eating well and getting enough sleep.
Plan in time for exercise and stick to this plan.

Copyright © Mometrix Media. You have been licensed one copy of this document for personal use only. Any other reproduction or redistribution is strictly prohibited. All rights reserved.

Beyond these techniques, there are other methods to be used before, during and after the test that will help the test-taker perform well in addition to overcoming anxiety.

Before the exam comes the academic preparation. This involves establishing a study schedule and beginning at least one week before the actual date of the test. By doing this, the anxiety of not having enough time to study for the test will be automatically eliminated. Moreover, this will make the studying a much more effective experience, ensuring that the learning will be an easier process. This relieves much undue pressure on the test-taker.

Summary sheets, note cards, and flash cards with the main concepts and examples of these main concepts should be prepared in advance of the actual studying time. A topic should never be eliminated from this process. By omitting a topic because it isn't expected to be on the test is only setting up the test-taker for anxiety should it actually appear on the exam. Utilize the course syllabus for laying out the topics that should be studied. Carefully go over the notes that were made in class, paying special attention to any of the issues that the professor took special care to emphasize while lecturing in class. In the textbooks, use the chapter review, or if possible, the chapter tests, to begin your review.

It may even be possible to ask the instructor what information will be covered on the exam, or what the format of the exam will be (for example, multiple choice, essay, free form, true-false). Additionally, see if it is possible to find out how many questions will be on the test. If a review sheet or sample test has been offered by the professor, make good use of it, above anything else, for the preparation for the test. Another great resource for getting to know the examination is reviewing tests from previous semesters. Use these tests to review, and aim to achieve a 100% score on each of the possible topics. With a few exceptions, the goal that you set for yourself is the highest one that you will reach.

Take all of the questions that were assigned as homework, and rework them to any other possible course material. The more problems reworked, the more skill and confidence will form as a result. When forming the solution to a problem, write out each of the steps. Don't simply do head work. By doing as many steps on paper as possible, much clarification and therefore confidence will be formed. Do this with as many homework problems as possible, before checking the answers. By checking the answer after each problem, a reinforcement will exist, that will not be on the exam. Study situations should be as exam-like as possible, to prime the test-taker's system for the experience. By waiting to check the answers at the end, a psychological advantage will be formed, to decrease the stress factor.

Another fantastic reason for not cramming is the avoidance of confusion in concepts, especially when it comes to mathematics. 8-10 hours of study will become one hundred percent more effective if it is spread out over a week or at least several days, instead of doing it all in one sitting. Recognize that the human brain requires time in order to assimilate new material, so frequent breaks and a span of study time over several days will be much more beneficial.

Additionally, don't study right up until the point of the exam. Studying should stop a minimum of one hour before the exam begins. This allows the brain to rest and put

Copyright © Mometrix Media. You have been licensed one copy of this document for personal use only. Any other reproduction or redistribution is strictly prohibited. All rights reserved.

things in their proper order. This will also provide the time to become as relaxed as possible when going into the examination room. The test-taker will also have time to eat well and eat sensibly. Know that the brain needs food as much as the rest of the body. With enough food and enough sleep, as well as a relaxed attitude, the body and the mind are primed for success.

Avoid any anxious classmates who are talking about the exam. These students only spread anxiety, and are not worth sharing the anxious sentimentalities.

Before the test also involves creating a positive attitude, so mental preparation should also be a point of concentration. There are many keys to creating a positive attitude. Should fears become rushing in, make a visualization of taking the exam, doing well, and seeing an A written on the paper. Write out a list of affirmations that will bring a feeling of confidence, such as "I am doing well in my English class," "I studied well and know my material," "I enjoy this class." Even if the affirmations aren't believed at first, it sends a positive message to the subconscious which will result in an alteration of the overall belief system, which is the system that creates reality.

If a sensation of panic begins, work with the fear and imagine the very worst! Work through the entire scenario of not passing the test, failing the entire course, and dropping out of school, followed by not getting a job, and pushing a shopping cart through the dark alley where you'll live. This will place things into perspective! Then, practice deep breathing and create a visualization of the opposite situation - achieving an "A" on the exam, passing the entire course, receiving the degree at a graduation ceremony.

On the day of the test, there are many things to be done to ensure the best results, as well as the most calm outlook. The following stages are suggested in order to maximize test-taking potential:

Begin the examination day with a moderate breakfast, and avoid any coffee or beverages with caffeine if the test taker is prone to jitters. Even people who are used to managing caffeine can feel jittery or light-headed when it is taken on a test day.
Attempt to do something that is relaxing before the examination begins. As last minute cramming clouds the mastering of overall concepts, it is better to use this time to create a calming outlook.
Be certain to arrive at the test location well in advance, in order to provide time to select a location that is away from doors, windows and other distractions, as well as giving enough time to relax before the test begins.
Keep away from anxiety generating classmates who will upset the sensation of stability and relaxation that is being attempted before the exam.
Should the waiting period before the exam begins cause anxiety, create a self-distraction by reading a light magazine or something else that is relaxing and simple.

During the exam itself, read the entire exam from beginning to end, and find out how much time should be allotted to each individual problem. Once writing the exam, should more time be taken for a problem, it should be abandoned, in order to begin another problem. If there is time at the end, the unfinished problem can always be returned to and completed.

Copyright © Mometrix Media. You have been licensed one copy of this document for personal use only. Any other reproduction or redistribution is strictly prohibited. All rights reserved.

Read the instructions very carefully - twice - so that unpleasant surprises won't follow during or after the exam has ended.

When writing the exam, pretend that the situation is actually simply the completion of homework within a library, or at home. This will assist in forming a relaxed atmosphere, and will allow the brain extra focus for the complex thinking function.

Begin the exam with all of the questions with which the most confidence is felt. This will build the confidence level regarding the entire exam and will begin a quality momentum. This will also create encouragement for trying the problems where uncertainty resides.

Going with the "gut instinct" is always the way to go when solving a problem. Second guessing should be avoided at all costs. Have confidence in the ability to do well.

For essay questions, create an outline in advance that will keep the mind organized and make certain that all of the points are remembered. For multiple choice, read every answer, even if the correct one has been spotted - a better one may exist.

Continue at a pace that is reasonable and not rushed, in order to be able to work carefully. Provide enough time to go over the answers at the end, to check for small errors that can be corrected.

Should a feeling of panic begin, breathe deeply, and think of the feeling of the body releasing sand through its pores. Visualize a calm, peaceful place, and include all of the sights, sounds and sensations of this image. Continue the deep breathing, and take a few minutes to continue this with closed eyes. When all is well again, return to the test.

If a "blanking" occurs for a certain question, skip it and move on to the next question. There will be time to return to the other question later. Get everything done that can be done, first, to guarantee all the grades that can be compiled, and to build all of the confidence possible. Then return to the weaker questions to build the marks from there.

Remember, one's own reality can be created, so as long as the belief is there, success will follow. And remember: anxiety can happen later, right now, there's an exam to be written!

After the examination is complete, whether there is a feeling for a good grade or a bad grade, don't dwell on the exam, and be certain to follow through on the reward that was promised...and enjoy it! Don't dwell on any mistakes that have been made, as there is nothing that can be done at this point anyway.

Additionally, don't begin to study for the next test right away. Do something relaxing for a while, and let the mind relax and prepare itself to begin absorbing information again.

From the results of the exam - both the grade and the entire experience, be certain to learn from what has gone on. Perfect studying habits and work some more on confidence in order to make the next examination experience even better than the last one.

Copyright © Mometrix Media. You have been licensed one copy of this document for personal use only. Any other reproduction or redistribution is strictly prohibited. All rights reserved.

Learn to avoid places where openings occurred for laziness, procrastination and day dreaming.

Use the time between this exam and the next one to better learn to relax, even learning to relax on cue, so that any anxiety can be controlled during the next exam. Learn how to relax the body. Slouch in your chair if that helps. Tighten and then relax all of the different muscle groups, one group at a time, beginning with the feet and then working all the way up to the neck and face. This will ultimately relax the muscles more than they were to begin with. Learn how to breathe deeply and comfortably, and focus on this breathing going in and out as a relaxing thought. With every exhale, repeat the word "relax."

As common as test anxiety is, it is very possible to overcome it. Make yourself one of the test-takers who overcome this frustrating hindrance.

Copyright © Mometrix Media. You have been licensed one copy of this document for personal use only. Any other reproduction or redistribution is strictly prohibited. All rights reserved.

# Special Report: Additional Bonus Material

Due to our efforts to try to keep this book to a manageable length, we've created a link that will give you access to all of your additional bonus material.

Please visit http://www.mometrix.com/bonus948/asp to access the information.

Copyright © Mometrix Media. You have been licensed one copy of this document for personal use only. Any other reproduction or redistribution is strictly prohibited. All rights reserved.